CASE STUDIES IN

CULTURAL ANTHROPOLOGY

GENERAL EDITORS

George and Louise Spindler

STANFORD UNIVERSITY

THE KWAKIUTL
Indians of British Columbia

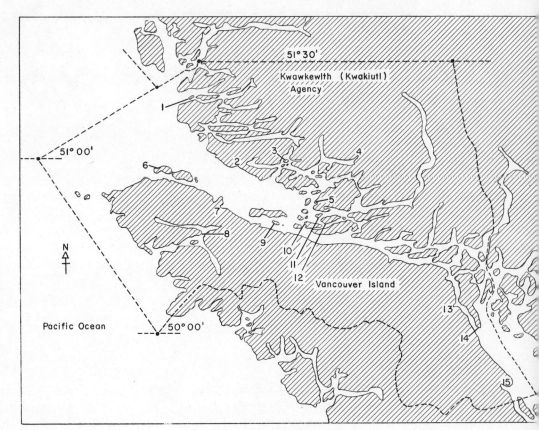

Location of Kwakiutl Reserves (see *Table 1*)

THE KWAKIUTL

Indians of British Columbia

By
RONALD P. ROHNER
and
EVELYN C. ROHNER
The University of Connecticut

HOLT, RINEHART AND WINSTON

NEW YORK   CHICAGO   SAN FRANCISCO   ATLANTA
DALLAS   MONTREAL   TORONTO   LONDON   SYDNEY

Copyright © 1970 by Holt, Rinehart and Winston, Inc.
All rights reserved
Library of Congress Catalog Card Number: 72–101691
0–03–079070–0
Printed in the United States of America
67890 059 9876

to our parents PRESTON, LETA, HEDY

The Proper Study of Mankind Is Man
                                    Alexander Pope

Foreword

About the Series

These case studies in cultural anthropology are designed to bring to students, in beginning and intermediate courses in the social sciences, insights into the richness and complexity of human life as it is lived in different ways and in different places. They are written by men and women who have lived in the societies they write about and who are professionally trained as observers and interpreters of human behavior. The authors are also teachers, and in writing their books they have kept the students who will read them foremost in their minds. It is our belief that when an understanding of ways of life very different from one's own is gained, abstractions and generalizations about social structure, cultural values, subsistence techniques, and the other universal categories of human social behavior become meaningful.

About the Authors

Ronald P. Rohner was born in Crescent City, California, in 1935. He received his B.S. in psychology from the University of Oregon in 1958, and he was awarded an M.A. and Ph.D. in anthropology at Stanford University in 1960 and 1964 respectively. Currently he is an Associate Professor of Anthropology at the University of Connecticut. In addition to a number of articles on the Northwest Coast, he is the author of *The People of Gilford: A Contemporary Kwakiutl Village*, and *The Ethnography of Franz Boas*.

Evelyn C. Rohner was born in Vienna, Austria. She was graduated from the University of Oregon with a B.A. in English, and she received her M.A. in anthropology at the University of Connecticut in 1967. She is the coauthor, along with Ronald P. Rohner, of an article, "Franz Boas and the Development of North American Ethnology and Ethnography."

Aside from their work among the Kwakiutl, both Ronald Rohner and Evelyn Rohner taught at the American School of Tangier, Morocco, where they were also the resident directors of the Moroccan dormitory in 1958–1959. In addition Ronald Rohner has done "ethnographic" research in a mental hospital on the West Coast.

About the Book

The visitor to present-day Gilford Island who has read of the massive plank houses which the Kwakiutl built so ingeniously that no sign of the joining of planks remained upon the surface, with colorful wooden crests representing family mythologies carved as totem poles and erected in front, would be jolted by the two rows of identical prefabricated houses on stilts, with nine outhouses for the 100 inhabitants (at peak season). He might be further jarred to see men dressed in ordinary working clothes and women in slacks. The Kwakiutl are today as they have always been, a fishing people; but they appear to live in a style similar to the White fishermen and loggers who also reside in the area.

In spite of these outward manifestations it soon becomes apparent that the people of Gilford Island are still uniquely Kwakiutl in the set of norms and values that guide their behavior. These norms and values are incorporated into a social system that has continuity over time, and that affords the people a sense of security and identity. Expressing generosity, borrowing and sharing, forming friendships, avoiding interference in the lives of others, and gaining power and prestige through interpersonal relationships are all valued. Though the extravagant potlatch where large amounts of material wealth were displayed and redistributed among the guests no longer exists, less ostentatious forms are still given which afford the host an opportunity to display his generosity, gain power and prestige, and validate his status.

The pattern of borrowing and sharing is an integral part of the behavior of the majority of Kwakiutl to the extent that a person cannot sink too low or rise too high. The Rohners call this the "subsisting oriented" category whose focus is on the present and on immediate problems. In contrast is a small group consisting of one household which the authors call "future oriented." This household has restricted social relationships and is little involved with the borrowing and sharing pattern of interaction.

The authors give an interesting account of the problems involved in teaching the children in a formal situation as Evelyn Rohner was contracted to do. Here the conflicts in values are magnified. The school represents a sharp discontinuity in the lives of the children. Learning by formal, verbal instruction is alien to them for they have experienced very limited structuring in their lives and are accustomed to learning by observing and performing. The Rohners were able to solve many problems by co-opting the parents, who were more than pleased to be included.

Drinking is the most popular pasttime in the village today. The Rohners estimate that time spent drinking often amounts to six full days per month. The personal goal of drinking is to get drunk or to drink until one "passes out" (goes to sleep). It is during periods of drinking that overt acts of aggression are committed. The Rohners see some positive contributions afforded by this aggression. In most day-to-day interaction expressions of discontent are circuitous and masked. Drinking releases inhibitions and allows people to express themselves more directly, thus improving the effectiveness of interpersonal communication. Drinking also seems to fill a void in the lives of the Kwakiutl created by the loss of traditional cultural forms. For example, when an intact traditional culture was functioning, the slack winter season was filled with ceremonial dances staged as dramatic theatrical productions. In order to convince the uninitiated that spirits were really present in the village the initiated used elaborate techniques of illusion to produce terror, drama, and comedy. "Prop" men hidden above the house beams manipulated strings that helped dancers control their magical tricks and supernatural birds flew through the air and appeared to carry off victims. A system of kelp speaking-tubes was installed and underground passages allowed dancers to disappear. These are only a very few of the accouterments used in the productions. There is little in the present, or in prospect in the immediate future, of the people of Gilford that rivals the excitement of their recent past. As in the case of most small non-Western cultures, subordination to the Euro-American system has meant much loss with little to replace what is lost. Nevertheless the people of Gilford Island have made a viable adaptation to conditions as they exist. Though to the casual observer there may be little to distinguish them from the non-Indian population, they have retained much of their social and cultural identity, and the current revitalization of some aspects of Kwakiutl life suggests that this identity will not soon disappear.

GEORGE AND LOUISE SPINDLER
General Editors

Stanford, California
September 1969

Preface

We begin this book with a word of explanation. Part One is written in the ethnographic present even though we lived in the Kwakiutl village on Gilford Island from September 1962 through August 1963, and again during June and July 1964. We have not been back since then, but from the letters we receive the village seems to have changed substantially since we left. Many of the people we describe, for example, no longer live there. Even though we have changed their names to protect their anonymity, the people and events described in this book are nevertheless real. Our effort has been to describe the distinctive quality of human life within the village at Gilford as it was when we lived there. Even though our presentation in Part One relates explicitly to one unique village among a series of unique Indian villages, Gilford is nonetheless representative of Kwakiutl communities. Most of what we write, therefore, can be generalized to *the Kwakiutl* rather than simply to the Gilford Island Kwakiutl.

Part Two describes some of the major characteristics of the traditional Kwakiutl social system including the rank-class structure, potlatches, and the impressive winter ceremonial. In many places we point out the basic alterations that have occurred in this system from the turn of the century to the present.

This book is intended largely for students. Our professional colleagues in Northwest Coast studies may take issue with us on certain points of interpretation, but since our goal is to capture the essential flavor of Kwakiutl life, we occasionally generalize without qualification beyond our firmly established data. We do this in order to maximize the fluidity of our presentation. Readers who want more empirical or quantitative documentation on the material presented here, especially in Part One, are encouraged to read the senior author's book, *The People of Gilford: A Contemporary Kwakiutl Village.*

We gratefully acknowledge the permission given to us by the Queen's Printer, Ottawa, to draw extensively from *The People of Gilford.* We also thank the University of California Press, the University of Chicago Press, and the University of Washington Press for permission to quote selections from copyrighted publications. In addition, we wish to express our gratitude to the University of Connecticut Research Foundation, especially to Mrs. Frances Hayward, for typing this manuscript.

R.P.R.
E.C.R.

Storrs, Connecticut
September 1969

Contents

PART ONE

Contemporary Kwakiutl

1

Fieldwork in Kwakiutl Life Space

Kwakiutl Life Space

LIFE FOR MOST KWAKIUTL INDIANS is confined to a slender strip of coastal water, fjordlike inlets, sounds, and hundreds of densely forested, almost impenetrable islands and outcroppings of rock between the western coast of British Columbia and Vancouver Island in Canada. Fifteen southern Kwakiutl Bands representing about twenty indigenous tribal groups occupy this territory between Smith Sound and Campbell River. One of these groups is the Gilford Island Band which is formally comprised of two closely related Kwakiutl tribal groups, the Koeksotenok and Hahuamis.[1] (See Table 1.) The residents of Gilford are the people described in this case study.

The Kwakiutl are today as they have always been—even in their mythology—a fishing people. Their self-identity is bound to the sea and to the life-forms within the sea. The great forests are exploited by white men, but only gradually and reluctantly are the Kwakiutl involving themselves in the logging industry. Agricultural enterprises are virtually unknown among the Indians. Some of the younger men take advantage of vocational training courses offered by the Indian Affairs Branch, and a very few go on for higher education. But ultimately many of them return to the sea, reaffirming a style of life that is as old as memory and tradition combined. Thus, even though the Kwakiutl are hardly the same people today as described years ago by the American anthropologist Franz Boas, important elements of cultural continuity with the past are nonetheless maintained.

---

[1] The Band legally consists of the Koeksotenok tribe, who traditionally occupied the village site, and the Hahuamis tribe. The Tsawatenok, a third Kwakiutl tribe, however, outnumbers either of the other two groups in the village. These three groups along with the Guauaenok form the Four Tribes of Gilford, an informally knit collectivity or confederacy who historically had exceptionally close contacts. Ninety percent of the residents at Gilford are members of the Tsawatenok, Koeksotenok or Hahuamis tribes. The Guauaenok are unrepresented in the community today. Most Tsawatenok, however, live on their own Reserve at Kingcome Inlet. Table 1 and the frontispiece map show the location of the various Kwakiutl tribes and bands.

3

TABLE 1.
TRIBES, BANDS, AND THEIR LOCATIONS IN THE KWAWKEWLTH (KWAKIUTL) AGENCY
(see frontispiece map)

No.	Band	Tribe(s)[a]	Location
1.	Quawshelah	Goasila	Smith Inlet
2.	Nakwato	Nakoaktok	Blunden Harbor
3.	Kwawwawaineuk	Guauaenok	Hopetown (Watson Island)
4.	Tsawataineuk	Tsawatenok	Kingcome Inlet
5.	Gilford Island	Koeksotenok and Hahuamis	Gilford Island
6.	Nuwitti	Nawiti (including Nakomgilisala and Tlatlasikoala)	Hope Island
7.	Kwawkewlth	Kwakiutl	Fort Rupert
8.	Quatsino	Quatsino	Quatsino Sound
9.	Nimpkish	Nimkish	Alert Bay
10.	Tanakteuk	Tenaktak	New Vancouver (Harbledown Island)
11.	Mamalillikulla	Mamalelekala	Village Island
12.	Turnour Island	Tlauitsis and Matilpe	Turnour Island
13.1	Campbell River	Wiweakam	Campbell River
13.2	Kwiakah	Kueha	Campbell River
14.	Cape Mudge	Wiwekae	Cape Mudge
15.	Comox	Qomox	Comox

[a] Spelling of tribal names follows Curtis (1915) with the exception of Qomox which is not included in Curtis. The Qomox are Coast Salish, not Kwakiutl.

Gilford Island itself is a mountainous land mass about 20 miles long and 13 miles wide. Nine mountains on the island rise over 2000 feet each, the highest stretching to almost 5000 feet. Steep slopes, sediment filled valleys and deltas separate the mountains. Rich needleleaf evergreen trees, bushes, fern, berry vines, and a wide range of wildlife cover the island. Different types of lush vegetation choke the often rugged and precipitous shore in their competition for sunlight. In many places the rising tide sweeps the stony walls of the island with the branches of the lower trees. This flora is sustained by a humid mesothermal forest climate, including about 54 inches of rain a year.

Marine life in the Gilford area is bountiful in its variety if not always in its yield. The waters are filled with clams, crabs, mussels, barnacles, varieties of cod, some octopuses and sharks, blackfish (killer whales), herring, halibut, oulachon, and five species of salmon.

The Indian village at Gilford snuggles against the base of one of the larger mountains that extends its slope to the shore. The community is about three times the length of a football field and about 100 yards wide. It is settled on an ancient clam-shell midden and is effectively bounded on three sides by dense forest and by water on the fourth. About twenty of the village houses are occupied continuously throughout the year. The others are usually locked or boarded by their absentee owners and comprise fair game for the vandalistic antics of village children.

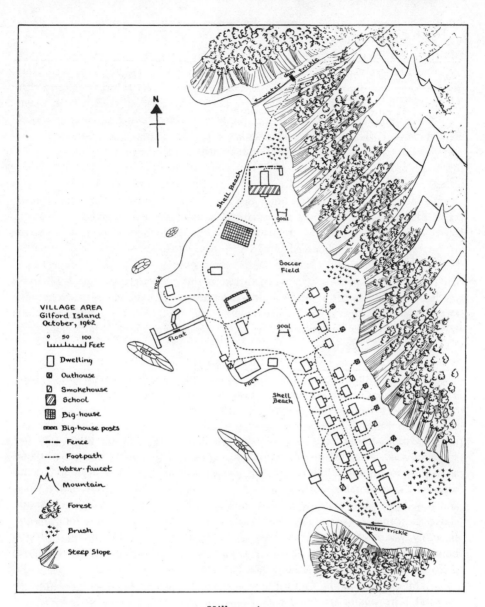

N

VILLAGE AREA
Gilford Island
October, 1962

0   50   100
└┴┴┴┴┴┴┴┴┘ Feet

⬜ Dwelling

⊠ Outhouse

⬘ Smokehouse

▨ School

▦ Big-house

▭▭▭ Big-house posts

—·— Fence

····· Footpath

· Water-faucet

⋀⋀ Mountain

Forest

Brush

Steep Slope

Village Area

The majority of the houses in the village, as well as the school and teacher-age, were acquired from a Canadian Air Force base in 1950. These identical pre-fabricated houses were transported to Gilford and arrayed on posts two feet off the ground in two neat, parallel rows on a newly bulldozed end of the village. Thus the disposition of houses at Gilford is exceptional among Kwakiutl villages in that their style and arrangement look like the suburb of a Canadian or American town.

The interior of village homes is thinly partitioned into a number of rooms of varying size. The kitchen and living room, for example, are unenclosed in Ambrose and Louisa Cedar's house, and their two bedrooms are separated from the living room by curtains that offer visual privacy but hardly mask sound. Their living room is sparsely furnished with a sagging overstuffed easy chair and a covered single bed that is used both as a couch and as a bed. Louisa has placed handmade crochet doilies over the arm and back of the easy chair, hiding some frayed edges. Plastic curtains are tied back from the windows; several windows are cracked and two are boarded. A wood-burning heater stands at one side of the room near a wall, and a Coleman lamp hangs from a hooked coat-hanger wire that is nailed to the ceiling. A worn linoleum rug covers part of the splintered, wooden floor. Louisa has several religious plaques and posters, family photographs, snapshots and a calendar neatly arranged on the wall near the couch. She also enjoys an arrangement of artificial flowers and several knickknacks on a shelf near the entrance to the kitchen.

The Cedar family eats around a Formica-topped table next to the kitchen windows overlooking the channel that bounds the village on one side. A short bench, a wooden chair and three soda-pop boxes surround the table, and a transistor radio that is rarely turned off rests on the windowsill next to the table. A large wood-burning range stands against the partition separating the kitchen from the living room. A rack used for both drying fish and for drying clothes hangs over the stove. Nearby a second gas lamp is suspended from the ceiling. One of the outside walls is lined with a counter in which a porcelain sink is embedded. Cold water that is gravity fed into the kitchen from a tiny dam on the mountain runs from the faucet, and the refuse from the sink drains onto the ground beneath the house. Not all houses in the village, however, have running water. Several families carry pails of water into their homes from one of the faucets protruding from several paths around the settlement. The nine outhouses in the village are shared by various families who normally lock them to keep un-authorized people out and to keep them from being damaged by mischievous children. A number of families use chamber pots for convenience at night.

The population at Gilford (about 100 people), as well as most of the other small, isolated Indian villages throughout the region, changes constantly. Individuals and sometimes whole families migrate easily from place to place among the local Reserves throughout the area, although an individual's strongest attach-ments are usually maintained with his home Reserve. Fluctuation of village size and composition are also influenced by marked seasonal variation. The village is practically deserted during the commercial salmon fishing season in the summer, but it fills again briefly after the summer fishing season ends. The size of the settlement is only moderately reduced in September after the residential school

Aerial and panoramic views of the village

children leave in the fall, but the age composition of the community is radically affected.[2] Population ranks swell again in the winter when members of other Kwakiutl Bands come to dig clams. Most of these visitors leave in early spring when the clam season is over. Finally, the village burgeons for a short time before summer fishing begins and after the residential school children return home.

Even within the village internal household shifts are commonplace. If one family leaves a house, a second often moves in, vacating its own home or leaving a host family to itself once again. Not infrequently this leads to conflict because the owners of the abandoned house may be unhappy about this intrusion. Moreover, young people often move or are moved within the village from one household to another where they live for indefinite periods of time.

Despite the residential instability of the villagers, the people spend most of their lives within the perimeter of an easily definable and circumscribed region. The psychologically real options for movement are restricted. The most extensive network of social relations for Gilford Islanders is localized among five other adjacent Indian villages—Kingcome, New Van, Village, Turnour, and the Bay.[3] When a Gilford Islander moves he usually goes to one of these villages.

The only way a person can travel in the region is by boat or pontoon plane;

---

[2] The Indian population of British Columbia was almost wiped out after European contact because of the introduction of diseases such as tuberculosis, measles and syphilis. Since 1939, however, the population has been burgeoning at an accelerating rate. Consequently 50 percent of the Indian population in British Columbia in 1963 was under sixteen and 75 percent was under thirty-two. The same trend holds true of the Gilford Island Kwakiutl: 50 percent are fifteen or younger and 75 percent are thirty or younger. Thus any alteration of the school-age population within the village seriously affects the character of the entire village.

[3] The full name of each village is Kingcome Inlet, New Vancouver, Village Island, Turnour Island and Alert Bay respectively, but we use these shorthand terms because they conform with the standardized usage of the Gilford Islanders.

A portion of the village as it looked in 1927 (Courtesy of the Provincial Museum, British Columbia)

consequently distance is typically reckoned in terms of the length of time required to get from one place to another by gill-net fishing boat, and not in terms of statute or nautical miles. Thus, Kingcome is about five hours away from Gilford. Village is about an hour away and New Van is approximately an hour and fifteen minutes from the village. Echo Bay, the closest inhabited place to the Indian village at Gilford, is forty-five minutes away and is on the same island. Simoom Sound is ten minutes further away on the other side of the cove from Echo Bay. Both Echo Bay and Simoom Sound are small, White settlements appended to Gilford Island on floats. Echo Bay has a general store anchored to the island as well as a provincial school and beer parlor on land. Other residents include forestry men and loggers who work for small, independent logging outfits. The settlement at Simoom Sound consists of a post office and general store built over the water where, along with the store at Echo Bay, the Indians buy many of their supplies.

Alert Bay with its paved roads and automobiles is the major commercial and social center of the entire region and is two hours from Gilford. The population of 1200 people there is evenly divided into about 600 Indians and 600 non-Indians. The Indian Agent's office is at the Bay along with two hotels, shops, beer parlors, fish canning companies, government offices, and the Royal Canadian Mounted Police (RCMP).

Indians and Whites in the Bay sometimes refer to the people of the more remote, isolated villages—such as Gilford—as "the islanders," and think of the island villages as being collectively depressed and conservative, whereas they view themselves as being progressive. Many Indians feel that living in Alert Bay gives them social and economic advantages not common to the remote villages. The islands are also thought of as being "tough places." Some individuals and families in these island villages share this negative evaluation of their village held by others. This, in part, accounts for the migration of families from the island Reserves to, most typically, Alert Bay. As a result, the isolated villages throughout most of the area are losing their population as families move to larger, more commercial areas. Quite frequently adults explain that they want to give their children a better education than is provided in the day schools situated on the island Reserves. This is often a legitimate reason; rarely, however, is it the only one. Not infrequently certain families complain about their home village, and state emphatically that they are going to leave as soon as possible. Some of these families have been threatening to leave for several years without acting on the decision or desire. Despite their disadvantages these traditional village sites still symbolize fundamental security and identity for many of the villagers. The village also provides for some of the older Indians a firm articulation with the fading image of a passing tradition. This is the life space of the Gilford Island Kwakiutl where our account unfolds.

Fieldwork in Kwakiutl Life Space

We did not specifically choose Gilford as our field station. We simply wanted a Kwakiutl village where my wife could teach while I conducted fieldwork; consequently the choice of community was made for us largely by the provincial

Superintendent of Indian schools. After we became settled and learned how to contextualize the village within the broader perspective of the surrounding Kwakiutl villages, however, we realized how serendipitous fortune had been. The village at Gilford is ideally suited in most respects for ethnographic fieldwork. It is small and compact, so we were able to have frequent and close contact with all of the villagers during the thirteen months of our residence. The size of the population made it possible for us to know everyone personally. Social life tends to focus within narrow boundaries because the community is isolated from other villages, and no one enters or leaves without others knowing about it. These are some of the structural characteristics of the village that make intensive fieldwork easier there than it might be elsewhere.

Before coming to Gilford we had expected a school enrollment of about twenty-five children in grades one to five, but on our first day Evelyn learned from one of the children that in fact she would be responsible for thirty-nine children ranging in age from six to nineteen and that she would be teaching every level from beginners through the eighth grade. The teacherage and classroom were in shambles when we arrived at Gilford because they were being renovated by carpenters hired by the Indian Affairs Branch. We cleared the sawdust and scrap lumber from one finished bedroom and part of the unfinished kitchen to set up living quarters. School was to begin in three days, but the classroom, books and supplies were in the same disheveled condition as the teacherage. Some of the supplies had not yet even arrived.

Evelyn was thrown completely off guard because she had not known that she was to be responsible for such a large class covering all grades. Moreover, she was dismayed by the fact that our quarters and the classroom were utterly disorganized and by the fact that many classroom supplies had not yet arrived. How was she to cope with all this in the three days remaining before school began? I helplessly watched as she became increasingly despondent over the teaching situation. Within two days she was almost completely withdrawn and apathetic. Her mood and attitude toward teaching changed several times every day, but remained essentially a feeling of futility and hopelessness.

Her unhappiness affected my own mood. I made no attempt to do systematic research during our first week at Gilford. I devoted most of my time to helping the carpenters complete their renovations, helping Evelyn prepare for class and making myself known within the community. I spent several hours each day probing around the village attempting to orient myself to it and to its inhabitants. I followed paths behind houses—which usually turned out to lead to outhouses—explored the beaches, and examined deteriorating totem poles, carved house poles and the big-house (traditional Kwakiutl multi-family dwelling), and I introduced myself to everyone I met. I felt I was being watched, so I attempted to make my actions as open as possible. I frequently engaged villagers in conversations and took notes on everything I saw and heard.

I was received with a mixture of curiosity and uneasiness which later turned to suspicion among a few villagers. My motives for being in the village were not clear. Evelyn was clearly the teacher, therefore her status was understood. She had legitimate work to do in the village, but what was I doing? Why was I there? Why was my wife working and not I? I attempted to establish myself as an anthropologist interested in the history, language and way of life of the people. My explanation satisfied no one because being an anthropologist is outside their existing lexicon of meaning. I felt threatened and insecure by this reaction, and I was disturbed because I could not explain my presence in the village in any way that made sense to the villagers. Within two weeks the resident Pentecostal deaconess confided to me that some of the villagers, especially the young men, had concluded I was a spy. My worst offense was public notetaking. "He's writing down all our secrets." Belatedly I stopped my open explorations and public note-taking.

Even though the school provided my wife—and later me—a secure identity within the village and allowed us to make progress in ways we would not have been able to do otherwise, the classroom posed the most immediate problem for both of us during the early part of the year. The children who had been shy and subdued at first became uncontrollably boisterous and inattentive in the classroom by the end of the first week. Evelyn discovered that the children were unresponsive to her attempts for eliciting group participation. She could not plan any activity involving the entire class. This aggravated the discipline problem created by the age differences among the students. The young ones became boisterous while she talked with the older ones, and the older students were bored and restless while she talked with the younger ones. The children tended to complete their assigned work perfunctorily, as quickly as possible, and they were not able to continue unguided to a subsequent task. A job which she expected the children to complete in fifteen minutes was indifferently completed by some in five. When a given assignment was finished, the children filled their time by talking, yelling, throwing things, scuffling, bickering and fighting. Evelyn found it impossible, for example, to coordinate the activities of each grade so that every child was busy while she taught reading to her beginners. She was unable to give her attention to one group without having children in another grade yell across the room, "Mrs. Rohner, I'm through! What can I do now?" If she did not respond immediately they began teasing each other or they pulled out their rulers and started a sword fight. When she did respond, the group with whom she had been working became restless and began to act up. By the end of the first week she was desperate, utterly discouraged and prepared to resign.

The following week she instituted a split shift system whereby children in grades one through four attended school in the morning and students in grades five through eight attended school in the afternoon. This resolved most of the problems created by a large class, but few of the classroom-control problems were ameliorated. Discipline and classroom control became increasingly difficult as the children became less inhibited in her presence. This was particularly true of the younger children.

By the third week the problem of classroom control approached such unmanageable proportions that we called a meeting of the parents in order to solicit their cooperation. Evelyn spoke to the parents about how important it was to her that the children learn; but, she argued, she could not be a policeman and a teacher at the same time. She described the problems of classroom management at some length, and then she explained the split shift and why it had been instituted. Most of the parents were in favor of the new system. We also explained to the adults that I had come to learn as much as I could about their history and about their way of life today.

During our coffee break several parents commented that this was the first time in the history of the school that the members of the community had been invited into the teacher's home for a meeting. Tears welled up in the eyes of one of the men when he told us this, and others concurred. Most of the teachers in the past had been distrustful of the Indians; several had been positively fearful or hostile toward them. Already, even before the meeting with the parents, we had unwittingly reduced some of the suspicion that the villagers had learned to hold toward new teachers by allowing the children and teenagers to visit us after school. But the fact that we invited the adults to our quarters was said to be novel in the recent history of Gilford. Certainly we had no way of suspecting beforehand that the parents-teacher meeting would be a major factor in our acceptance within the community.

The story was told the day after the meeting that I had been especially hired to write about the people of Gilford. Few villagers understood exactly what this meant, but they were proud that Gilford had been chosen. The role of anthropologist contained too many ambiguities for my behavior to be clearly understood or predictable, however, so I was cast into the status of *the teacher* even though everyone realized that Evelyn was actually in the classroom. My status as the teacher meant that I was in charge of the school and that, presumably, my wife was working for me.

Several people during the parents' meeting mentioned that a movie projector and screen belonging to the village had been in the Indian Agent's office for ten years. They complained that the Agency Superintendent refused to return the equipment. I said that I would talk to him and see if I could reclaim it. The idea was warmly received but, based on their past experience with Whites, several people believed I would not really try. Two days later I accompanied four men to the Bay and retrieved the projector and screen. Several young men from the village who had been very suspicious of me earlier travelled back to Gilford with us the same day. They accepted me into their conversation for the first time, and when we arrived at Gilford they invited me to join a beer drinking party with other villagers. Throughout the evening I was asked to recount how I reclaimed the apparatus. Our period of probation in the village ended. We were no longer required to prove ourselves in the same way. Other problems of adjustment and rapport arose throughout the year, but the one of general acceptance was largely settled.

We barely escaped the network of mutual grievances which is a normal part of village social interaction, however, because of our attempts to actively participate in community life. The most serious event occurred during our third month at Gilford. The tribal chief accepted me into his trust and confidence and loaned me his gill-net fishing boat, the *Dorothy Rose*, for the winter, thereby giving me priority over some of his kinsmen who had no boat. The chief had earlier admitted to me that he was reluctant to have the village men use the *Dorothy Rose* because they often damaged it. He had difficulty collecting the repair bills. "Sometimes I think they expect me to pay them for using my boat." Within two weeks a few villagers began resentfully complaining that the chief had loaned me the boat rather than some of his relatives who needed it for clam digging. The women were most voluble in their complaints, primarily to my wife. Fortunately the antagonism shown to us was limited to only a few villagers.

Chief Stanley Philip gave me explicit instructions not to loan the *Dorothy Rose* to anyone. I was to be responsible for it. The evening after the chief left the village with a load of clams for Vancouver, however, one of the village men told me that Stanley had instructed him to take the *Dorothy Rose* to a nearby trap line and pick up another villager. I was disturbed that the chief had not told me about this before he left, and I was not certain that Stanley had really instructed him to take the gill-netter. I wanted to keep my promise about not loaning the boat if Stanley had not made the request, but I did not want to offend the villager if he had. Stanley later admitted that he had instructed his son, Herbert, to take the boat. Herbert did not want to go, so he asked another villager. Stanley said that he would not ask anyone to use the boat again as long as it was in my charge. The next time he left the village Herbert asked for the keys, saying that he needed to take a load of iced fish to Alert Bay. Again, I did not know if this were true, but I hesitantly gave the keys to him anyway because I did not want to offend him by refusing his request. This was particularly true because he and his wife appeared to resent the close working relationship I had with his father. Repeatedly on other occasions Herbert said that he needed the *Dorothy Rose* for apparently legitimate purposes when his father was away.

We were in a position where we were constantly forced to make decisions about the use of the *Dorothy Rose* without having adequate knowledge of the proper normative standards by which such decisions should be made. The standards used by the villagers for evaluating appropriate use and control of property were not the same as the ones we were using, and it became apparent that neither Stanley nor the villagers perceived our use of the boat in the same way as we did. In effect it was free for us to use whenever it was not needed for other purposes; but who, I wondered, was to be responsible for maintenance, repairs, equipment, gas and oil? I believed that I was fully responsible for these when I accepted the boat, but I had no way of controlling them when it was used by others. I raised the question of responsibility with Stanley but he did not give me a satis- factory explanation. I later realized that the question was meaningless, based as it was on my implicit assumptions about the meaning of responsibility rather than on those held by the Gilford Island Kwakiutl.

During this time I reached a plateau in my fieldwork. The amount of in- formation I was getting in relation to the amount of time I was spending to obtain it was decidedly dropping, and I felt I was drifting aimlessly. I had become habituated to the routine of village life and I was developing few insights and hypotheses for testing. Problems regarding the *Dorothy Rose* bothered me. And I was troubled by my relationship with Herbert, who had begun calling me

"Riley" and "Riley Rohner." I asked him what he meant the first time he said it and he explained, "You're leading the life of Riley." He saw me talking to, watching and working with the villagers, but he had no clear idea of what I was doing, so he perceived my activities as loafing. His joking caught me at a time when I was feeling particularly vulnerable in my relations with some of the men.

At about this time we began to feel the need for a vacation from the island—a chance to get away and take a look at ourselves and the village. Both of us were getting too caught up in village affairs and this was creating a great deal of strain and tension in us. When we left the village for two weeks at the end of December, with Stanley's approval we gave the boat keys to Herbert, who reluctantly returned them when we came back. He intermittently used the boat during the next few weeks. Tension regarding the *Dorothy Rose* increased when Herbert came by one day asking for the keys to the boat to go to Simoom Sound and pick up some crab pots. He had told me previously that he wanted the keys to put out Stanley's crab pots, but Stanley knew nothing of it when Evelyn mentioned it to him. I mentioned this to Evelyn who got angry because Stanley had told her that "There's no reason for Herbert to be using the *Dorothy Rose* now that the clam tide is over." The problem reached a climax a few days later when I asked Stanley why only one oar was on board the gill-netter. Two pairs had been locked inside the cabin when we left the village at the end of December. He gave me a penetrating stare and informed me that Herbert had said three oars were missing when we left. It was my word against his son's. All three of us were in an awkward position, but Stanley faced the greatest dilemma. Somehow he had to reconcile his feelings toward me, whom he liked and respected, with his paternal feelings and obligations toward his son. Shortly thereafter I relinquished responsibility for the *Dorothy Rose* in order to avoid further conflict.

We saw less of Stanley for a month. Herbert and his wife became much friendlier after the problem with the *Dorothy Rose* was settled and when they no longer had to compete with us for Stanley's favor. Herbert and his wife, Gertie, invited us to their home many times in the remaining months and we reciprocated. Eventually we became good friends. Herbert's wife wept when we left the village after a year of fieldwork, and a few weeks later she wrote to Evelyn, "Well I can't tell you how much I miss having you pop in any time of the day to visit me. I think I won't become friendly with anyone again as I hate good-bys, you know everyone here hated to see you all go. Well, I'd like to just say that you are *the* very best friend I've ever known, so there."

Anthropologists often pose a threat to people who feel their vested interests in a community are being disturbed by the work of the ethnographer. We posed such a threat to the resident Pentecostal deaconess because of our extensive participation in village life. The deaconess, Hilda, is a knowledgeable woman who helped us a great deal in getting oriented to the village and the surrounding area. She eased many of Evelyn's early problems of adjustment, and she supplied me with invaluable data, the absence of which would have made the initial months of research more difficult. Later, however, she felt insecure because of our involvement in community affairs. One afternoon she talked to two villagers, Henry and Norma, and chided Henry for drinking too much. Henry retorted that we, "the teachers," do not "talk bad" about the Indians' drinking and that in fact we drink with them ourselves. Hilda was angered by this comment and replied that she had nothing in common with us and that the only reason I drank with the villagers was to get information for my book. During parties throughout the remainder of the year, and during our revisit the following summer, I was confronted with the question, "Is it true that the only reason you drink with us is to get information for your book?"

A more hostile incident occurred when we were drinking beer on Herb's boat one evening and then moved to Patrick's place. Henry and Norma were in bed drinking. Norma was in a foul mood. She told us to get out of her house—"This isn't the Ritz, you fucking bastards." At one point she commented to the effect, "You'll have something else to put in your book, you spy." She was looking at one of the other men when she said it, but the comment was obviously directed toward me. She was equally as unpleasant to her brother, Pat. Most people, however, admitted that they did not really believe we drank with them merely to get information.

Throughout the year we voiced our approval of the perpetuation of customary Kwakiutl traditions and technology such as barbecuing salmon and clams, carving, painting and Indian dancing. The people of Gilford were pleased when we displayed with pride the contemporary artifacts we purchased from them, and they were flattered by our interest in their history and customs. Chief Philip spoke at length during several ceremonial dances about the work I was doing, and how my constant probing had renewed in him and others a fading interest in Indian customs. During one occasion, for example, he said, "I would like to publicly acknowledge my debt of gratitude to my esteemed anthropologist friend, Mr. Ron Rohner, for rejuvenating my long-lost interest in old Indian customs."

By mid-school year we received a letter from the Superintendent of Indian schools in which he wrote:

> What scares me is the vacuum that you will leave when you go South. The sympathetic involvement that has taken place since you arrived will be missed greatly. My grapevine has been most complimentary to you, but I do not think that complimentary is too accurate. The Indians are a bit overwhelmed but like what is going on. All the reports that have come to me have been good and this was to be expected. Too few try to understand; too few listen; too few care.

One of the young men who had been most distrustful of my activities during the year paid us the highest compliment, however. On our last day at Gilford he said to us, "I never was proud of being from Gilford until you came." We received many letters from the villagers after leaving Gilford. In one of them Stanley wrote, "We the Gilford Islanders will always remember you folks. You have left quite an impression on the Peoples."

Our feelings about the village are expressed in a letter that Evelyn wrote two months before we returned home:

> I have to laugh in a way. Last September I wanted nothing more than to go home. If there had been a convenient way of leaving this remote village, I probably would have done it. Now look at me. I love it and I am really sad that we will not return

next September. Of course there have been bad moments, moments of extreme homesickness on my part, times of extreme frustration on Ron's part. But what a wonderful ending to a year, a village in which feeling is good, a community that is functioning together.

As you can see, the Rohners have become extremely involved in their new home. I am thankful that we will be able to spend the summer here. Many of the people have expressed regret that we will not be back next year; Ron and I also feel that way.

2

The Kwakiutl at Work

Two Days in December

THE VILLAGERS GO TO BED between ten and eleven on school nights and they get up between eight and nine in the morning. The sharply defined time segments so important to White teachers, however, are ignored by villagers on weekends and during school vacation. This led us to believe that the Kwakiutl prefer to guide their lives according to events such as when they *feel* tired or *feel* some other pressure rather than to be locked into an arbitrary set of habits imposed by alien and intrusive institutions. Prescheduled events, except school, rarely begin at the designated time because few families start getting ready until it is time for the activity to begin. Both Indians and Whites sometimes refer to this orientation as "Indian time."

The day usually begins with breakfast of tea and toast, or occasionally hot chocolate or cereal. Children are sent off to school at nine and the workday begins, although schedules are so diversified depending on the week, month or season that an accurate, composite description of daily life is difficult. Men may go to the village float to work on their gill-netters—repairing the engine, pumping out the bilge, or drawing the boat onto the high tide beach to be scraped or caulked. Some men stand around idly talking to their neighbors or work on their torn nets.

Willis Drake, the chief councillor in the village, goes at least once a week to Simoom Sound and Echo Bay for supplies for his store in the village. He also picks up the village mail as well as supplies and mail for the school. People often hop a ride with him to get some of their own groceries and mail, including Unemployment Insurance Checks (UIC) and relief checks, or they send a note with Willis asking for supplies, generally on credit. Credit for subsistence needs is basic to the livelihood of the Indians. Since they rarely have ready cash available, a great strain would be put on them if merchants refused credit. The storekeepers know members of the community well enough to make decisions about the extension of credit; moreover, the store owners at Simoom Sound have an effective

17

technique of forcing payment from negligent villagers. They run the area post office in which checks are received; sometimes, if a family is too far behind in its payment, the storekeepers do not forward the money. Rather, they send a note saying that the check is being held for them. With the money in his hand the debtor finds it hard not to pay at least part of his bill. A comparable technique is used by Chief Philip when he functions as the clam buyer on the clam scow. He automatically deducts debts before he pays his clam diggers. Credit is categorically refused at the beer parlor in Echo Bay.

I asked the store owner at Echo Bay about the relationship between Indians and Whites regarding the payment of bills. He explained, "Whites are either black or white as far as their credit is concerned. Either they pay their bills well or don't pay them at all. Indians, on the other hand, may pay well for awhile and then stop paying anything at all; later they may pay again." Overall, however, he feels that Indians are a better credit risk than Whites: "Many Whites take off when they owe me too much and never return. Indians almost always return to the area where their kinsmen live. In the long run it's often easier to force payment from Indians than Whites."

After Willis leaves the house in the morning, Lucy, his wife (as well as the other wives) straightens her house, washes the dishes and perhaps begins heating water for laundry. A few hours are usually required to get enough hot water to fill the large galvanized tubs. Several of the women have access to gas-powered washing machines, but others use scrub boards. While they are waiting for the water to heat they may relax at the kitchen table overlooking the channel and listen to their transistor radios, or begin preparing salmon or clams to be barbecued for a later meal. The villagers at Gilford do not have refrigerators so the preservation of perishable food is sometimes a problem. They have learned that barbecuing, smoking and drying are moderately efficient means of keeping marine life from rapidly spoiling. At one time they immersed foods such as wild berries in closed containers of oulachon oil, thus sealing out the air and preserving the fruit, but few people do this today. Barbecued clams, as the term is used at Gilford, are clams that have been removed from their shells, laced onto skewers and placed in front of an open fire to cook and smoke for an hour or two. The same method is used to barbecue salmon: a fish is filleted, secured within a stake frame and placed around a fire. Fish and clams for smoking are either placed on racks in a smokehouse and left for a day or two with a continuous smoky fire inside, or they are dried on racks over a small open fire and left in the sun or on a rack over the kitchen stove to dry further.

By the time the women have gotten well into these chores children and men are home for dinner. The midday meal is generally the largest of the day and may consist of stew, macaroni, wieners, sandwiches, clams or fish, and canned corn or some other cold, canned vegetable. The Kwakiutl almost inevitably include tea and bread with their meals. Potatoes too, are very common; they eat rice less frequently. Fish, barbecued clams and boiled potatoes are dipped into a bowl of oulachon grease which is in the middle of the table. Serving dishes are placed on the table and each person reaches for what he wants. Villagers eat few fresh vegetables and little fruit. They almost never drink milk, although they use canned milk in coffee. One woman calls fresh produce "White man's food." Occasionally, especially after a night of heavy drinking, they eat eggs and bacon. At least one meal a day typically requires the use of a spoon as the basic implement, but those meals consisting of fish and potatoes are eaten with the fingers. If anyone is hungry after a meal or between meals, he eats bread.

Meals are typically eaten quickly and almost in silence. Noisy or talkative children are admonished to be quiet. Whatever conversation occurs follows the meal over a cup of tea. Many of the families supplement their regular diet by trading food items. One family may give venison to another, and later, the second reciprocates with some other food such as fish. Leftovers are thrown to the village dogs, but when excess food is scarce the dogs forage for themselves. After dinner, the men go back out or take a nap and the children return to school.

Malnutrition, according to local medical personnel, is one of the most prevalent health problems among the Indians. Gertie, daughter-in-law of Chief Philip, was amazed when a doctor told her that she could eat three meals a day, feel satisfied and still not receive the nutrients she needs for good health. Because of malnutrition the Kwakiutl are susceptible to infectious disease of all kinds, including tuberculosis. Dental problems are also attributable to diet. Chronic anemia is yet another common health problem, and obesity in middle age is one of the most notable physical characteristics of the people.

Each family is responsible for securing its firewood. The Drakes, for example, are low on wood so Willis takes his gill-netter to get a log he saw drifting in the channel last night while he was jigging for cod and other bottomfish. After Willis relocates the log he lashes it to his boat, tows it back to the village, floats it onto the beach at high tide, and then sections it with a chain saw. Some of the other men cut logs by hand unless they can borrow a chain saw. The round sections are carried to a woodpile beside the house and split into four large pieces. All this is man's work. Either men or women chop one of the large pieces into kindling or into a size appropriate for the stoves.

The division of labor among the Kwakiutl is neither sharp nor crystallized, although certain jobs are customarily assigned to men and others are allotted to women. Men are responsible for most commercial and subsistence activities; women tend to the majority of the domestic chores. With notable exceptions men do not cook in the home, nor do they wash the dishes, but they do both when they are fishing. Women wash clothes and complete the little ironing that is done. Both men and women clean the house, but this is viewed as largely women's responsibility. Fishing of all types tends to be largely man's work even though men, women and children dig clams. Many women cannot read a tide table; consequently most of them are dependent on men for making decisions about when and where to dig. Women with the help of children usually dig clams for family use. More men dig clams for cash than women.

School is over at three in the afternoon. Willie Moon's parents are in bad credit-standing at Lucy and Willis Drake's store because they have been derelict in paying their bills. Edna Moon, Willie's mother, forgot to order bread, margarine and canned lunch meat when Willis went to Simoom Sound this morning, so after school she sends Willie with a note to the Drakes' store asking for these groceries rather than face Lucy herself. The Drakes stock only fast moving items in their back room such as candy, eggs, bread, canned milk, margarine, soda pop, canned lunch meat and occasionally fresh fruit. They also handle the village dispensary which contains ointments, aspirin, bandages and other first aid and medical supplies, for which they receive ten dollars a month from the Indian Health Services. The Drakes keep no written records of their income from the store, but they maintain a clear mental record of the debts and credits involving most people in the village. Lucy refuses Edna's request for supplies and makes several pointed remarks to Willie about people not paying their bills. She is confident Willie will repeat these remarks to his mother. Lucy has sent five notes to the Moons' home in the past two days saying, "I know you have the money. Please pay." Dunning through the use of notes carried by children is common among Gilford villagers. The adults who are dunned avoid going to the store because, as commonly expressed, "they are ashamed."

Forcing payment of debts is a frequent problem in a wide variey of situations. David Crow, a young shipwright in the settlement, for example, built a rowboat for another fisherman who delayed payment for many months. "Finally I flipped my cork," David scowled, "and gave him until the twentieth to pay or I'd take the boat away." Moreover, David feels that he is losing friends in the village by extending credit for work and then trying to collect. His father has admonished him on numerous occasions never to work on credit, "but only now am I learning the truth of what he said." Not uncommonly several years lapse before payment is made, and then it is made only after energetic insistence on the part of the creditor.

After Willie returned home with his verbal message and another dunning note from Lucy, he and three village adolescents forage around the village for beer bottles which they collect in preparation for shipment to Vancouver. Each case contains twelve bottles and is worth fifteen cents in the Bay or twenty-five cents if it is sent directly to Vancouver. On one occasion the village youths collected two hundred seventy cases of bottles; six months later several adults crated two hundred cases. This gives a rough but minimal approximation of the amount of beer consumed in the village during that time.

By the time Willie and his friends return home supper is ready. Supper, a lighter meal than dinner, consists essentially of the same foods. After supper Edna and her three kids put on their gum boots, hats, sweaters and caps, grab their clam forks, a couple of pails, one of their gas lamps and a pronged stake on which to hang it. They go to the low tide beach off to one side of the village to dig clams for tomorrow's dinner. Many village residents dig on the beaches adjacent to the village for family food but they do not often select these beaches for commercial digging because too many people have exploited them for too long. Paul, Edna's husband, joins half a dozen other men and a scattering of women who are congregating on the scow and on their boats. They plan to dig commercially. Two boats left for distant clam grounds over an hour ago to get there before the tide reached its ebb, but Paul and his companions do not plan to go as far. They are going to the west side of Mars Island, about twenty-five minutes from Gilford.

Before they leave, Paul and two other men go aboard the scow to pick up their gunnysacks. Paul needs a new clam fork because the handle of his old one cracked the last time he was out, and one of the other men needs some naphtha (white gas) for his Coleman lamp. The cost of the fork will be deducted later from Paul's clam sales. The radiophone behind the counter crackles and occasionally erupts with a noisy message between two seiners in the area. The radiophone on the scow provided the people's only immediate link with the outside world during our year at Gilford, but since then a permanent one has been installed within the village.

The official clam season typically opens on November first and at this time Chief Philip tows a scow to Gilford from a fish company in the Bay. The scow is tied alongside the float, and from the first day it becomes the business and social center in the village. It is possible to find men congregated on it or on the float beside it almost every day. Stanley Philip is the official clam buyer but Herbert or one of Chief Philip's other sons operates the scow while Stanley makes his daily rounds of neighboring villages and clam sites to buy clams from those people who cannot get to the scow. Gilford is commonly thought of as the clam center of the region and, for this reason, many Indians migrate to the settlement for varying lengths of time during the winter. The villagers and the visitors at Gilford dig most of the clams that are purchased on the scow.

The groups of diggers who typically travel together to clam sites remain fairly constant. The person who owns or has access to a gill-netter decides where to go and as many as seven people accompany him. The people assembling on the float with Paul, however, represent a potpourri of diggers who do not belong to any such semi-stable group. Paul is not happy about the prospect of digging this evening because the tide is poor—villagers usually begin digging at a 5-foot tide even though this is not considered a good one—and the temperature is dropping noticeably. Digging continues each day through the low point of the tidal period, or simply "the tide" as the Kwakiutl call it, and digging stops when the low tides have risen back to 4 feet.

By the time tides are at 4 feet it is late at night because corresponding low tides are approximately fifty minutes later each day. Low tide on the first digging day of the 1962–1963 season, for example, was at 5:37 P.M. Six days later at the end of the tidal period (most tidal periods are about ten days with an average of eight intervening days between periods), it was 10:00 P.M. The Indians rarely dig if low tide is after 11:30 or 12:00 P.M. because the yield in a 5-foot tide is characteristically much lower than in a 1-or 2-foot tide, and because the time during which they can dig is greatly reduced. For these reasons fewer Indians dig during 4- and 5-foot tides than during lower ones. Furthermore, most of the appropriate clam tides before February occur after dark, but by March and April some midday tides occur, and sometimes the tide goes low enough to dig twice each day in February and March—once in the morning and then again twelve hours later in the evening.

Paul's enthusiasm for this evening's work is diminished further as the clam crew approaches its destination because the wind is beginning to spring up. The Kwakiutl dig at night, in the rain and not infrequently in near-freezing weather; but they do not, as a rule, dig during periods of high wind. Gill-netters are usually anchored in a cove near the clam beds and the clam crew rows to shore in a dinghy that has been towed behind the gill-netter. High winds may cause the gill-netter to be swept onto shore or into the open water of the channel, or the row boat used to go between boat and shore may be swept away when the tide begins to rise. In either case diggers can be left stranded and their boats may be lost or destroyed. Paul is also concerned that the breeze will push the water too far onto shore, thereby keeping the tide—as poor as it is—from reaching its predicted low. Pat Cedar wrote about this regarding the 1963–1964 clam season, "Well. sure bad this year for clam digging. not so hot to much wind or two small of a tide. but I guess it will pick up soon."

After they arrive on Mars Island the men go their individual ways several yards apart and search for the best place to begin digging. Experienced diggers believe that digging is most productive when the tide begins to flow. The reasons given for this vary. Some say that the clams come closer to the surface as the tide rises; others say that it takes them most of the tide to find a good clam bed. Willis Drake, Gideon Amber and Jacob Abel are recognized as being outstanding diggers. These men are said to know exactly where to dig at each site, whereas most people have to search for a productive clam bed.

The clams are placed in a pail; when the pail is filled it is poured into a gunnysack which, when full, weighs approximately 60 pounds—equivalent to "a box." The box is the standard unit of measurement for clams. Clams are supposed to be poured from the sacks into clam boxes and then back into bags. A good digger can produce six boxes in an evening, but the average person digs only three or four.

Clams very often are not measured when the diggers sell them. But the men working on the scow informally assess the weight of each sack as it is thrown from the gill-netter onto the scow and into a corner. The clams are measured in clam boxes, however, some time before they are shipped to Vancouver. Chief Philip has one of his sons perform this task while they make the buying rounds of the various villages and clam sites. He measures clams not to check the weight of each sack, which experienced handlers can tell quite accurately by lifting the bag, but to check the contents. Some diggers put rocks, sand or other heavy objects in the sacks to increase the weight, or they deliberately do not fill the sack to an estimated sixty pounds. Stanley was incensed when the chief from a neighboring village did not quite fill his sack. As a precautionary measure some clam buyers weigh every sack, but this is very time-consuming. A second reason for transferring clams from one container to another is to examine and sort the clams themselves. Badly damaged clams and horse clams are thrown overboard. Moreover, government regulations specify that certain kinds of clams must be a specific size before they can be sold. For example, butter clams may not be less than $2\frac{1}{2}$ inches across, whereas razor clams may not be less than $3\frac{1}{2}$ inches across, and littleneck clams must be at least $1\frac{1}{2}$ inches across.

After enough clams have been collected on the scow, Stanley hauls them in his seine boat to Vancouver, about a day and a half from Gilford. He usually needs to make two trips each tidal period because clams spoil quickly. Rarely do clams remain on the scow for more than four or five days. By the end of the 1962–1963 season Stanley had taken nearly 11,000 boxes (well over half a million pounds) of clams to Vancouver. This only accounts for the clams that Stanley personally picked up from nearby sites or that had been delivered to the scow at Gilford. The fishermen were paid $1.80 a box (three cents a pound) for clams during the 1962–1963 season, but the price varies from time to time. The following season, for example, the Indians refused to dig for Chief Philip until his company matched the $2.50 price offered by an independent buyer. When the fishermen began digging for the independent buyer, Stanley's company reconsidered and paid the $2.50 a box.

After Paul and the other diggers leave for their clam site, Pat Cedar and Charlie Bean row almost a mile to Bonwick Island in a borrowed, hand-hewn canoe. They have a .22 caliber rifle, a shotgun and a high-powered flashlight with them. They row quietly along the shore of the island beaming their light on the bank and into the brush, searching for deer. Deer are attracted to the light, and the reflection from the deer's eyes is easily visible and provides a fair target at close range. Pit lamping—the use of a spotlight at night—is illegal, but it is the most effective, and thus popular, means of hunting. Occasionally men also hunt in logged-out areas during the day. The official deer season runs from the middle of September to the end of November, but in practice the official season makes no difference to the Indians. The men hunt throughout the year, especially for deer, but also for other animals such as ducks when they are available. The Kwakiutl are allowed to get a permit to hunt for food outside the formal season, but they rarely bother to obtain one. In fact many of them are not aware that they are eligible for permits. A deer is dressed where it is shot to make it more easily transportable. It is skinned, quartered and butchered in the village and the meat, known simply as deer meat, is used for stew. We once invited Gertie and Herb Philip for a venison steak dinner, but they were unable to eat the meat because they have so many missing teeth.

By the time Pat, Charles, Paul and the other clam diggers return to the village it is nearly midnight. About half the diggers pause on the scow after selling their clams to buy a piece of pie, a hot dog, a cup of coffee or a pack of cigarettes from Gertie Philip, who has set up a small business there. The others go home to have a snack before retiring—coffee as a treat, but more often tea, plus bread or crackers, margarine, jam and sometimes other foods such as dried fish.

Henry Rochelle, a white man allied to one of the village women in common-law marriage, is a logger. He and Daniel Drake, Willis Drake's half brother, are the only men in the village who regularly log rather than fish. They leave the village at seven each morning in Danny's speed boat. Although some of the other men also log for brief periods of time, especially during the low income months of April and May when they have less to do than during any other time of the year, logging is not popular. In fact a few Kwakiutl express fear of working in the woods. Frank Bean, for example, described his work in one of the local camps and concluded that he is afraid of logging but that he needs the job. "I have to pull my share in the work or be a coward," he confided.

Logging in the "gyppo" or "gyp" outfits, as the small logging companies

Artistic representation of two ceremonial dance figures (Allen James)

are locally known, is sometimes dangerous, but it is probably no more so than some of the other jobs the Indians regularly perform. Danger is hardly a sufficient reason to explain the reluctance of the men to work in the woods—except that the Kwakiutl more readily perceive the risks there because they are not at ease in the forest. A more important reason for their reserve about working in the

Salmon hunter dance (Allen James)

lumber industry is that logging often requires them to be away from the village and from their families except on weekends. They are willing to do this for a few months, but seldom for longer. Moreover, the logging camp nearest Gilford is said to be understaffed, thus each man must perform jobs that normally require two or three men in the larger operations. Indians have the reputation among logging employers of being valuable and hard workers, except that they very often do not get to work on time. If they have been drinking or if some important social event is taking place, they frequently do not show up for work at all. A few of the men have a long history of being fired from jobs because of this.

Other men are just getting out of bed as Henry and Danny leave for work. Ambrose Cedar is in his early fifties, overweight and has a bad heart so he cannot fish or log anymore. Over the years he has become an extraordinary artist and craftsman. He makes his living largely through carving, but this modest income is supplemented by family allowance and an occasional relief check. Pat, his nephew, has a badly curved spine which Pat attributes to being pushed down a cliff; but it is the opinion of a local doctor that his hunched back is more likely due to tuberculosis as a child. Pat can do no heavy physical labor, and relies largely on art for his small income. He has watched his uncle carve and paint all his life and under this tutelage has become a capable and rapidly maturing painter. Jeffrey Hardy, also a brilliant craftsman, is the third village resident who gains most of his livelihood from a commercial craft. A few of the other men in the village also carve during their free time. The work of each of these men follows traditional themes. Ambrose and Jeffrey produce such artifacts as stylized ceremonial masks and hamatsa (cannibal society) whistles belonging to the traditional winter ceremonial dance societies. Pat often depicts dancing figures in their ceremonial costumes and scenes from these winter dances.

Craftsmen usually sell their products to the store owner at Echo Bay, but they sometimes ship them directly to dealers in Vancouver. The price paid for masks carved by different men varies greatly, reflecting not only the difference in quality but also the minimum price that some of the novices will accept. Jeffrey complained to me with annoyance that the "beginners are selling their masks cheap and bringing the price down on good ones."

Some basic changes have taken place in Kwakiutl crafts over time, mainly through the influence of Whites. Carving and painting are being transformed to suit the demands of the commercial market, or at least to match the Indians' perception of such demands. Traditionally, but essentially true today too, men worked with rigid materials such as wood, not excluding cedar bark. Women worked with pliable material, making cedar bark cloth, for example. Today women crochet, knit, embroider and make "shiny paper" pillow covers from the foil in cigarette packages. None of these have much commercial value but are used to decorate homes and are given away at potlatches.

The people are losing a large part of their traditional technology as they become increasingly dependent on industrially produced goods. At one time they manufactured fishing nets from the fiber of nettles; now they buy nylon nets. They once produced adhesives from the translucent tissue between the skin and flesh of the salmon; they now use glue and tape. They used to utilize natural elements in the environment to produce colored pigments for their oil base paints, but today they buy commercial enamels. Furthermore, relatively few younger people are able to cut and strip fish into thick pieces as they once did. Gertie Philip was annoyed and embarrassed when a group of older women found her experimenting with the technique of barbecuing salmon. The older women know the technique but she did not, and she admitted that she was "ashamed to ask them."

Ambrose is disgruntled this morning. He has had few requests for masks recently and he is almost broke. Louisa, his common-law wife, is sick; and yesterday his request for relief from the Indian Agent was denied. Ambrose's reproachful reaction to being turned down for relief is a typical one. Through the paternalistic policy of the Indian Affairs Branch, especially until recently, many Indians have come to expect assistance from the Agency as part of their natural right. Ambrose is doubly discontent, however, because some of the other villagers have recently received relief, and he feels that his need is at least equally as great as theirs. He went on to cite several people who have extra sources of income—for example, Harold Dick who has a trap line—and who nonetheless receives relief, whereas he—who is without such a supplementary source—has been refused. Villagers often become resentful when someone else receives welfare assistance, regardless of the need, and they do not.

Not infrequently Indians ask the Agency Superintendent for relief when they have been drinking or when they are inebriated. The Superintendent turns

Village woman making a clam basket

down all such requests, except under exceptional circumstances, asking, "Where did they get the money for liquor if they need relief?" Some Indians are almost automatically granted relief assistance when they apply for it because the Agent believes they never ask unless the need is real. He believes he has to use caution in filling other requests. Many Indians are reported to regularly give misinformation about their income when they apply. Similarly, the Indian Agent believes that he cannot necessarily trust the recommendations of the village band council because of the strong kinship bonds within the community and the resultant bias. On rare occasions a band councillor argues with a kinsman and refuses to recommend him for relief when it is genuinely needed; sometimes councillors recommend relief even though there is no real need.

Before sunup this morning, David Crow left the village in his gill-netter to try his hand at salmon fishing with his new trolling poles attached to the boat. He spent the past day and a half on the float, assembling equipment and stripping bark from long, straight, tapered saplings to be used as trolling poles. This is the first year that trolled salmon have been purchased on the scow. This is also the first time that most of the men are using trolling poles; in the past they trolled by hand. David and the other men who are attempting to master this new technique have had to learn from Whites and other commercial trollers about the type of equipment to use, how to assemble it and how to use it. A man sometimes leaves the settlement for two or three days between clam tides when he trolls with poles, but he rarely needs to stay away for more than a day when he trolls by hand. David is not sure how long he will stay out—perhaps a couple of days if he is successful but, if not, he plans to return home this evening. A number of men in the winter of 1963 viewed trolling with poles as more of a novel pastime than a serious occupational enterprise. Even though the price for trolled fish is fairly high, the small catch and the expense of running the gill-netter reduce the profit and often result in a loss.

Several hours after Dave left, Harold Dick and his common-law wife, Jennie Drake, set out separately from the scow, Jennie in Harold's canoe and Harold in a borrowed row boat. Jennie is going to jig for family food and Harold intends to check his trap line. Jennie is an obese woman in her fifties who speaks very little English. She knows more than any woman in the village about traditional technology and she is the only woman we observed going out alone in a boat to fish. Moreover, she is the person to whom others turn for information about basket weaving, making button-blankets (ceremonial dance blankets) and dance aprons, barbecuing clams or smoking halibut; she is also the reluctant village midwife. Jennie has been legally married twice. Her first husband, who is the father of Willis by another wife, died. She left her second husband and lived with another man until he died. Then Harold moved in with her. She has had fourteen children by these men, and the majority of the Gilford Island Kwakiutl with the surname of Abel (her maiden name), Drake, Bean, Crow or Dick can trace very close kinship affiliation with her. Furthermore, she is related to well over half the villagers if kinship calculations are extended to include bonds through marriage. But then, from this perspective almost all of the Gilford Islanders are related in some way to one another.

Harold's trap line lies along the northern perimeter of Bonwick Island across from Gilford. About 500 feet from Bonwick he spots a hair seal coming up for air. He raises his shotgun, fires, and swiftly rows to the spot where the seal is flailing in the water. He drags the dying animal onto his boat, kills it, expertly cuts off its nose, and then tosses the carcass back into the sea. The Game Commission has established a bounty of $5 per nose for hair seals because they attack salmon trapped in gill nets.

Hal continues on to check his line for mink and otter. He spent three days last month setting out his line; it takes him half a day to check it. Hal has his shotgun with him because if he spots a free animal he intends to shoot it—regardless of where he sees it or on whose line he happens to be. Pelts of animals that have been shot are often badly damaged and therefore less valuable than the pelt of trapped animals, but even a damaged pelt is worth more than none at all. Harold has a widespread reputation for poaching, that is, for shooting or stealing animals on the trap lines belonging to other men. Joe Abel, Jennie's brother, has had a lot of trouble with Hal poaching on his line. He describes Hal as a "real haywire guy, a real orang-utan." Although he has never pressed charges against Hal, poaching is in fact punishable by a heavy fine and/or jail sentence. Indians rarely lay charges against each other, even if one actually catches someone poaching on his territory. This attitude is characteristic of the Kwakiutl in most situations and is described more fully later.

Jennie has been home for a couple of hours by the time Hal returns. She caught so many fish that the light chop caused by the afternoon breeze combined with her own weight caused water to wash over the gunwales of her canoe. Her canoe was barely afloat by the time she reached Gilford. On the float she filleted half a gunnysack full of fish and left the remainder in the canoe. On the way to her house at the far end of the village she told people to take as many fish as they wanted. Most people took two or three, but one woman took a gunnysackful. Fishermen take what they need, share the excess and tighten their belts when the fishing is poor, since on many occasions fishermen return home with no fish at all.

These events illustrate two days in December. They do not begin to exhaust the complete range of activities in which the Kwakiutl involve themselves during other seasons. As revealed in Table 2, for example, winter gill netting opens before the trapping season closes at the end of February. The price of netted spring salmon during this time is considerably reduced from the trolled price of the same fish earlier, because the fish tend to be bruised or damaged as they are drawn back onto the boat.

Between these two seasons is the period of oulachon fishing for domestic household use. The people of Gilford fish for oulachon during March and April in the Kingcome River. Oulachon are also plentiful at the head of the Knight Inlet, about a day's travel from the village, but few Gilford Islanders go there. Traditionally certain tribes had fishery rights at specific locations, but not at others. Such rights on the Kingcome River were shared by the Four Tribes of Gilford (Koeksotenok, Tsawatenok, Guauaenok and Hahuamis), as well as the Nimkish and the Komkyutis. Other tribes shared Knight Inlet. Today these rights are not carefully

TABLE 2.
SEASONAL ECONOMIC AND SUBSISTENCE ACTIVITIES[a]

Sources	Length of Activity by Month											
	Nov.	Dec.	Jan.	Feb.	Mar.	Apr.	May	June	July	Aug.	Sept.	Oct.
Summer Salmon Fishing							—	– –				
Clam Season				– –	– –	– –						
Halibut Fishing					– – –	———	———	———	——	– –	––	–
Winter Trolling	———	——	—									
Winter Gill Netting				——								
Trapping												
Oulachon Processing					—							
Deer Season		– –	– –	– –	– –	– –	– –	– –	– –	– –	– –	– –
Duck Season		– –	– – –	–	– –							
UIC		——	———	———	———	———	——					
Seaweed Collecting							—					
Family Allowance												

[a] The broken lines in the table indicate, for example, that the summer commercial salmon season opens in May, but the Kwakiutl at Gilford do not begin intensive fishing operations until the latter part of June. The clam season formally opens in November and closes in May but the villagers usually quit digging commercially in the middle of March.

guarded and members of different tribes may go to different places; nonetheless, a strong tendency persists to fish at traditional sites.

Oulachon, which are related to smelt, are netted, placed in earth pits, and allowed to partially decompose. The oil content of the fish is so high that the fish may be used as candles by simply drying them and inserting wicks in the dried carcass. After rotting for ten days they are placed in a large vat of boiling water which causes the oil to rise to the surface. The oil is scooped from the top of the water and is bottled in gallon jugs. Skill and experience are important in making oulachon oil, or "grease" as the oil is customarily called. Those people who do not have the expertise to manufacture it usually buy it from someone at the currently standardized price of $5 a gallon, although at times it is given away, primarily to close relatives or friends.[1] Grease is a staple in the diet of many families and is usually eaten with fish and boiled potatoes. It is also used as a

---

[1] The 1968 price was reported to be ten dollars a gallon.

medicine (rubbed on the body to reduce fever), and it figures prominently in feasts and potlatches (public display and distribution of property in the context of one individual or group claiming certain hereditary rights or privileges vis-a-vis another group).[2]

The months of March through May are among the most economically diversified as well as socially active. They are also the months when the people of Gilford have the most free time. Clam digging closes, winter gill netting opens and closes, the oulachon run passes, halibut fishing opens, and by the time it closes the commercial salmon fishing season opens. In addition, the Kwakiutl take advantage of special seasonal products such as berries, seaweed, crabs, and sometimes barnacles. Crabs are collected in spring on the low tide beaches or in shallow water. A few men put out crab pots. People occasionally eat barnacles after they are collected and steamed free from large chunks of rock. This is rather rare, however, since many people now are unaware that barnacles are edible. Berries are collected primarily by children during the late spring and early summer. In May adults travel a day's journey to sites where seaweed grows. It is picked, dried for several days on top of the big-house or sometimes on specially constructed platforms, and each night it is re-collected and stored in a warm, dry place. Fresh water such as dew or rain is said to spoil it. After the seaweed is dry it is finely ground and stored in containers. Seaweed is considered as something special to be eaten as it is or put into clam chowder or on cold canned corn.

The majority of the village men define fishing—especially salmon fishing—as their most important economic activity. Clam digging is less important for most Indians than fishing, both in their over-all life process and in their self-definition. This is true even though they spend almost an equal number of days throughout the year doing both. Many men could earn a great deal more money through logging, but they choose not to. None of the men during our year at Gilford could remember exactly how much money he had earned the preceding year in logging, clam digging, crafts or trapping; but many of them could recall quite closely how much money he earned from fishing (mean $1700; range $400–$3200). We interpret this as an indication of their close identity with fishing. Furthermore, there were ninety days in which people could dig clams during the 1962–1963 season. Given the fact that the diggers produce an average of at least three boxes of clams per tide per person, one could expect their mean personal income from clams that year to approach $500. In fact, however, the average (mean) income from clam digging during the 1962–1963 season was $200 or 60 percent less than expected. This too reflects the people's more casual attitude toward clamming. With these facts in mind we turn now to the commercial salmon fishing season.

Commercial Salmon Fishing

The Native Celebration in Alert Bay, or June Sports as the occasion is more popularly known, takes place during the last week of June each year. It informally marks the beginning of commercial salmon fishing even though the season

---

[2] We discuss the potlatch at greater length in the last chapter.

officially opens earlier. Although some men fish before the close of June Sports, the major event marking the season is the annual salmon run north in the area of Rivers Inlet, about a day's voyage. The opening of the fishing season at Rivers Inlet coincides with the celebration of June Sports.

The Kwakiutl Indians fish on two types of boats—gill-netters and purse seiners. The mechanics of gill-net fishing are quite different from purse seining. In the first place, gill netting is a one- or two-man operation, whereas seining requires a crew of four to seven men. More importantly the style of fishing is totally different on the two types of boats. Different kinds of nets and other equipment are used. Seiners fish during daylight hours (in the early summer from 4:00 A.M. to 10:00 P.M.) whereas gill-netters can fish equally well during the day or night. The process of netting the fish on seiners bears no relation to netting fish on gill-netters. In the latter, the gill net (from which this type of fishing takes its name) is managed from a drum anchored toward the stern of the boat. When a fisherman arrives at his chosen fishing grounds he drops his net out into the water through rollers secured off the stern. The boat is positioned down wind from the net so that the craft does not drift back into the net.[3] Once the net is out both the boat and the net are allowed to drift. Fish swim into the net and try to pass through but they cannot because the mesh is too small. Then they try to withdraw and in the process their gill covers become entangled in the net. Periodically the fisherman rolls his net back onto the drum, disentangling the salmon and other fish that have become caught as the net passes over the rollers. The task of bringing in the net takes about ten minutes if it is empty but it takes considerably longer if fish and debris are caught in it.

Gill-net fishermen at Rivers Inlet are extremely competitive with each other. Benny Otter described fishing at Rivers as "a panic." Potential conflict between seiners and gill-netters is reduced in the Rivers area because only gill-netters are allowed in the inlet itself. Gill-netters fish at night in areas where both may work, thus avoiding mutual interference. Nonetheless, violence or the threat of violence is reported to sometimes erupt.

During intervals between net checks, the gill-net fisherman sleeps, reads or listens to his radio; if fishing has been very poor he may make one set and leave it until morning. But the men usually sleep very little during the night at Rivers Inlet because of the large number of fish that swim into the net and because of the dangers of drifting into one another's net. Men who damage the net of another fisherman are responsible for making reparation. Moreover, a sleeping gill-net fisherman runs the risk of having his net or boat drift into a restricted area. Fisheries Department boats and planes carefully patrol the areas and levy a fine against anyone who has allowed his net to cross a restricted boundary.

A packer boat from one of the three fish-packing companies based in Alert Bay usually collects fish from the Gilford fishermen at least once a day. Each boat flies his company flag as identification for the packer. Occasionally,

---

[3] Gill nets, which vary in size and color, are suspended vertically in the water by a cork-line attached to the top of the net causing it to float, and by a lead-line at the bottom weighing it down. They vary in length from about 200 to 300 fathoms (1200–1800 feet) and they are usually 2 fathoms deep.

Village fisherman disentangling a salmon. The net in the water is supported by the cork-line behind the gill-netter.

however, depending on the area, the fishermen take their fish to a buyer stationed on a scow near land. The men are expected to sell their fish only to the company for which they work. No money actually passes hands except when a fisherman sells his fish to an independent buyer for cash; independent buyers often pay more than the fish companies. The men recognize that selling to independents is a risky practice, however, because they are dependent on their fish companies for credit, for financing boats, for nets and other equipment, and for a steady market. The companies extend credit at the beginning of the season for food and for supplies, and they perform other services as well. Part of a man's commercial success depends on his reputation with one of the fish-packing companies. A fisherman who is caught selling his fish to an independent buyer may lose favor with his company, and this can create a major hardship.

Purse seiners are much larger than gill-netters, and seining is done during daylight hours. Seiners carry large nets which are designed to be manipulated by two boats—the seiner itself and a skiff. The nets are typically 125–200 fathoms long and 9–10 fathoms deep. And as is true of gill nets, the top of the seine net is supported by a cork-line and the bottom is weighted by a lead-line; a purse-line is connected by rings to the lead line. The seiner crew may attempt to set the net to surround a school of fish; or the men may simply make set after set in an advantageous position, sometimes waiting several hours to take a turn at a good tie-up spot on the shore. The salmon are trapped when the bottom of the net closes and forms the purse. This is why this form of fishing is called purse-seining. Seine boats hold a set open for twenty minutes, the period of time authorized and enforced by the Fisheries Department.

A seiner crew is usually composed of four to seven men. Shares are computed on the basis of seven-man crews, but when seiners go out with a short crew each man receives a greater part of the profit. A full crew typically consists of the skipper, one cook, three men on the deck of the seiner, and two skiff men. Profits are divided into eleven shares, seven to the crew, and the remaining four go to the boat, the net and the skipper. The net and boat shares are taken by the owner of each, very often a fish company. The cost of food, fuel and some equipment is deducted from the gross earnings before shares are apportioned. If the seiner damages someone else's or its own net, this too is deducted from the gross earnings. Many skippers do not allow their crew to inspect the books. In this way the skipper can sometimes include deductible items that his crew would find objectionable, but the crew seldom shows any concern for what is deducted from the gross earnings before their shares are allotted. Some crews suspect their skippers of cheating, and for this and a variety of other interpersonal reasons the crews on most seine boats continue to change throughout the fishing season.

Most men at Gilford prefer to own or at least operate their own gill-netters rather than sign on as crew members of a seiner. One of the village men, Victor Philip, expressed the sentiment of many others when he explained why he prefers having his own gill-netter: "I'm my own boss. Some guys on seiners are real haywire and others get stuck doing all the work." Most of the village men, including older adolescents, have worked at one time or another on a seiner, but most of them agree that they can make more money by operating their own gill-netter—if they can get one. They catch fewer fish but they also have fewer expenses. Only one person receives the earnings—but he must meet the costs, too. None of the men at Gilford skippers his own seiner during the commercial salmon season.

Several of the village fishermen have had their own gill-netters in the past, but they had them taken away by the fish companies and now they work on seiners. A couple of the villagers, for example, mortgaged their boats to a fish company for nets costing about $1000 each. The men neglected to make payments on the nets and, as a consequence, they lost both their nets and their boats. The Indians understand why the nets were taken from them but they do not understand why they lost their boats. They do not realize the implications of a mortgage. The transaction was both honest and legal from the fish company's viewpoint, but the villagers see the Whites as cheating them. Chief Philip summarized this kind of problem with the observation, "Indians today don't have the business sense they used to have. They used to be good."

Fishing is a risky venture and it is becoming increasingly uncertain each year as more people enter the industry with more efficient equipment and as the provincial government enforces stricter limitations on the times and places where men can fish. One of the complicating factors in the fishing economy of the Indians, for example, and one which is creating a great strain on the economy, is the restricted fishing week. In the past, the fishing week extended from 6:00 P.M. Sunday to 6:00 P.M. Thursday. Toward the end of the 1963 fishing season the week was reduced to a two-day period beginning 6:00 P.M. Sunday and closing at 6:00 P.M. Tuesday. Occasionally the fishing week is extended a day or two, but far more often it is not. Although commercial salmon fishing is open from May to October, the most productive fishing tends to occur from the end of June through early August. Thus, the effective fishing season for the people of Gilford is about three months. Fishing closures are determined by the Fisheries Department as part of their conservation program. Fairly tight controls must be maintained at the northern end of Vancouver Island where the Kwakiutl live in order to protect the fishing interest of men further south, as well as to assure that enough salmon reach their spawning grounds.

The Fish Commission notifies fishermen of impending closures by radio broadcast. Seiners have a radiotelephone on board, but most gill-netters do not. Those people who do not have a radiophone are notified through the informal communication network of other fishermen and fish packers. Many people keep their transistor radios or radiophones tuned to the marine frequencies for fishing information. Listening to marine bands on transistor radios and use of radiotelephones to intercept messages have major implications for communication throughout the area. Few bands on the radiophones are restricted; consequently anyone who is interested may listen to conversations between boats or between ship and shore. This explains, in part, the celebrated "Indian grapevine" by which many people know about events as soon as, or even before in some cases, the people who are involved. Radiotelephones are used extensively by the fishermen to exchange information about fishing. Fishermen are often secretive about their location if they are discussing good fish catches because they know that others are listening. In fact Indians often speak Kwakwala, the native language of the Kwakiutl, in order to exclude at least non-Indians from this information. The radiotelephones are also vital to notify others of an accident or of a breakdown.

Boats travel from place to place searching for fish or move from an area which has been closed to one type of fishing, for example, net fishing, to another zone that is not restricted to net fishing. Although experienced fishermen usually know where fish are likely to be found, they also travel on the basis of personal and overheard conversation. Certain localized areas, such as the entrance to streams, are permanently closed to fishing. Other areas may be temporarily closed to gill netting or seining but may be left open to trollers.

A man's catch in certain places and at certain times is heavily dependent on the kind of fishing he is doing. Trollers may do well at one location, but not seiners or gill-netters. At another time in the same place seiners may do best. The type of equipment a troller or gill-netter uses also makes a difference. Troll fishermen experiment with different types of lures in a single location, searching for the most effective one. Since they are dependent on the fish seeing and being attracted to the lure, they must fish during daylight hours. Gill-netters try to use a net that is virtually invisible to the fish. Weather conditions such as intense sunlight, fog or wind influence the visibility of nets. As a result, the gill-netter with a light green net may be more successful at one particular time than a boat with a darker colored net, and so forth. Many of these variables are unpredictable, although certain rules generally hold true. These and many other factors combine to make commercial fishing an uncertain occupation.

Unanticipated events such as strikes called by the fishermen's union can impose even greater hardships on fishermen. The 1963 season, for example, was one of the worst that many of the Indians could remember because of a strike lasting from July 13 to August 3. The strike took the heart out of the fishing season, and it was compounded by additional closures and a scarcity of fish after the initial salmon run at Rivers Inlet.

Even though the brief Rivers Inlet run is usually the most productive part of the season, many of the men feel no sense of urgency to leave right after June Sports. Only a minority of the Gilford Islanders left immediately for Rivers in 1963. Most of them returned to Gilford for several days to make their final preparations. Those men who left right after June Sports were able to sell their fish before the strike began, but those who returned to Gilford were hurt the most. The former made from $200–$500; the latter made nothing.

Most of the gill-net boats from Gilford remained at Rivers after the strike began on the assumption that it would end in a few days. By the time it was finally settled, the majority of the villagers had returned home. Even at that time many families were beginning to feel a strong financial pinch. The men complained that they would rather fish at a reduced price than not fish at all. Some of them were resentful that the channel by Alert Bay was teeming with salmon and they were not able to go after them except for family food. Almost all the fishermen left Gilford the day the strike ended; seiners arrived to pick up their crews and the gill-netters traveled independently to the fishing grounds, but fishing was relatively poor throughout the remainder of the season.

Most families immediately felt the impact of the strike, because few maintain capital resources on which they can draw in an emergency. Moreover, almost half of the families at Gilford habitually rely on such administrative sources of income as relief, unemployment insurance and family allowance to supplement their income. Except in extreme cases, however, villagers were not eligible for relief from the Agency during the strike because the government could not be in a position to support the strike. Furthermore, the strike created a long-range hardship in that few of the fishermen were eligible for unemployment benefits during the winter because they had not been able to meet the requirement of a minimum of fifteen weeks of fishing.

We received several letters from villagers in the fall of 1963 expressing their feelings and attitudes toward the season. "the fishing is very poor the last few weeks," wrote Patrick Cedar. "O. well thats part of life I guess. you got take what you get and give what you got. Well its not that bad. good old winter will soon be here. go clam digging and so." The attitude of passive acceptance expressed in his letter is familiar among the Kwakiutl. The same theme was reiterated in a letter several weeks before the fishing season ended by Willis Drake, who wrote, "Fishing hasn't been good at all with all this fog were having. and the ten day closure we had. were going out to-day for four days and we heard there'll be another closure after this. Oh well I guess it can't be helped." Gertie Philip concisely revealed the economic hardship imposed by the poor fishing during the season with the statement, "Fishing was worse than poor, some gilnet fishermen even had to have welfare help."

The effects of the strike were minimally ameliorated because the clam season opened a month earlier during the 1963–1964 season than it normally does.

Pat Cedar wrote to us about this at the first of October. "Well the fishermen have it real bad. no fish at all. they having two week tie up. But do you know [Stanley] buying clams now. he doesnt [usually] come until Nov. But he's here. the digers just coming in so clam diging mite be better than fishing yet." However the consequences of the fish strike were not as severe as they could have been—at least from a basic subsistence point of view—because during the strike the Indians could fish for family food. On one occasion during the fishing season a seiner from a neighboring village came to Gilford with 1900 salmon. They left 400 on the float and distributed the remainder among three other villages in the immediate Gilford area. Each family took as many fish as they could carry. Some people even filled a row boat, but shy or unassertive people were left with few fish. Those villagers who took more than their share were sharply criticized. Large quantities of salmon such as this are usually home-canned as well as smoked and barbecued.

3

Being a Kwakiutl

E VEN THOUGH MOST OF THE VILLAGERS at Gilford are physically identifiable as Indians, they look and dress very much like the other fishermen and loggers throughout the area. Herbert Philip, for example, is twenty-eight, 5 feet 10 inches tall with black hair which he wears in a long crew cut. He wears colorless plastic rimmed glasses and although he still has all his front teeth, a canine is missing along with a few molars. Herb usually wears working trousers, a sport shirt, work jacket and cap. He is not noticeably overweight yet, but in a few more years he will be. His wife, Gertie, typically wears slacks and a well-washed blouse or short sleeved Orlon sweater. Occasionally she wears a house dress. Her flat shoes are badly worn and they are beginning to break down at the sides.

Both Herb and Gertie are reticent, emotionally reserved, soft-spoken, shy in front of strangers, and passively oriented toward life. Of the two, Gertie has a quicker temper and becomes very angry when she is irritated—for example, when she feels that Herb is not getting a fair deal. Shortly before the end of our year of fieldwork, for example, a chartered yacht tied up at the float. The teenage son of one of the yachtsmen invited Gertie and Evelyn, who had been strolling around the village, aboard for a brief visit. Early the next morning the skipper banged on the Philips' door and superciliously requested Herb to accompany him in a row boat to some spots where the skipper could catch crabs. Herb, in his agreeable fashion, went with the skipper. A few hours later he returned home carrying a can of Dinty Moore beef stew, four brass nuts and some bolts as payment. Gertie was outraged. She was annoyed with Herb for accepting the junk, as she called it, and she was infuriated with the skipper for insulting her husband. As she said to us that evening, "Who does the fucking bastard think us Indians are anyway? Herb went with him because he's a nice guy, not because he expected to be paid. And that crap isn't pay anyway."

Herb, as is typical of most of the villagers, has a fair sense of humor about himself and his own weaknesses, and he enjoys telling jokes about Indians and

Whites. One of his favorites is a story concerning the difference between Indians and White men: Indians scalp their enemies but White men skin their friends. A second anecdote relates to the interaction between an Indian and a White man in the city. A White man approached a bus stop where an Indian was standing and smugly said, "I'll give you a dollar for every question you can ask me that I can't answer, and you pay me fifty cents for every question I ask you that you can't answer." The Indian thought it over for a moment and agreed. "And to show you how fair I am," the White man continued, "I'll let you ask the first question." The Indian meditated for a moment and asked, "What has two heads, the body of a wolf, two tails and eight legs?" The White man was startled by the question and finally grudgingly pulled a dollar bill from his wallet, giving it to the Indian. At that moment the bus arrived and the White man hurriedly asked, "Well, what is it?" The Indian handed the White man fifty cents and stepped onto the bus.

The Kwakiutl are no longer exceptional because of their economic activities, their religious practices and beliefs, their social or ceremonial life, their house style or the food they eat. In most ways, in fact, they live in a style very similar to the White fishermen and loggers who also reside in the area. Therefore the Indians can be viewed as a rural, working-class, subcultural variant of the North American class structure, rather than being a distinctive cultural group.

What then makes the Kwakiutl unique today as a culture-bearing population? To be a regularly participating member within the social system at Gilford, in a very broad sense, implies a status with its associated role(s)—as demonstrated by the fact that the villagers maintain a definite set of norms that guide their behavior and by which they evaluate the behavior of each other and outsiders.[1] It is these norms and valued behavior standards that give life within the village at Gilford a large part of its distinctive flavor. Individual decision-making processes are guided by these norms as are interpersonal relations, and aspects of the Indians' world view. These norms and values also give a fair amount of stability and continuity to village life over time. That is, social systems survive only insofar as the constituent roles (which imply the maintenance of socially legitimated and recognized normative standards) are performed, and they are performed largely because they satisfy personality needs. Thus, the individual's motivation to continue performing the roles is provided. In this way the requirements of the social system are met in that the social roles continue to be performed, giving appreciable stability and continuity to the system, and simultaneously many personality needs are also satisfied. From this point of view, the subcultural system at Gilford has a double-edged quality about it insofar as individuals must adjust to the valued behavior standards if they are to live comfortably within the village, but at the same time, these standards supply the

---

[1] In our usage a status is a social position that is defined independently of its occupant. The test condition of a status is the question, "Are norms attached?" If the social position is not defined by a set of norms then it is not a status, and every social position that is defined by a set of norms is a status.

conditions for villagers to make a personal adjustment. A sense of security, a reference group for personal identity, and social approval are provided for those who adhere reasonably well to the normative standards. On the other hand, the villagers impose compelling and often subtle negative sanctions on the person who violates norms too extremely or too often. These sanctions are effective, of course, only for those Indians who are motivated to remain within the system.

Social Control and Normative Standards

Through at least minimal contact with Whites for over one hundred years, two general acculturative classes have developed among the Kwakiutl. The most prevalent is the *subsisting oriented* class and the second is the *future oriented* class. Subsisting orientation implies a focus on the present—on continued existence or the condition of subsisting at a day-to-day level. A central characteristic of this class is the need to cope with life in its immediacy, as it actually presents itself, rather than to strive to create some new form for an indefinite future. Villagers in the subsisting oriented acculturative category prepare for the predictable, anticipated or known future, but they generally do not plan for the remote or unknown future. Villagers tend to cope with the way things are now rather than attempt to change them. Men gather logs and cut them for firewood; they catch fish which are sometimes canned or dried for use in the winter. These activities are forms of preparation for a predictable future. Rarely do villagers plan, however, if planning is understood as thought and effort given to some long range goals which are considered to be at least potentially realizable. Consequently families rarely save money or other goods for some unknown exigency. Thrift and saving are not included in the value system of people in the subsisting oriented class. Individuals who conform to the same set of characteristics as the subsisting oriented, except that they tend to look to past traditions as being as good as, if not better than, contemporary living, are *past oriented*. This acculturative class is a special case of the subsisting oriented category. Almost invariably these people are fifty years old or more. This attitude is rarely shared by the younger Kwakiutl. With a major exception noted below, the Islanders tend to be characterized as subsisting oriented.

No individual who remains in the subsisting oriented web of interaction within the community can sink too low or rise too high, either economically or socially, because of the patterns of borrowing and sharing. Borrowing and sharing have sharp leveling effects and occur from an interaction between personal choice and social obligation. Items are borrowed (often permanently), given, exchanged and freely taken among members of the community. An individual or family in need may borrow from another who has a surplus. Requests are sometimes refused, but consistent refusal sets an individual apart from the remainder of the community and disrupts normal social relationships. It also directs criticism against the person who refused. An individual who accumulates material wealth and is interested in maintaining close social ties in the community must be prepared to share his wealth. But since they know that they may have to redistribute their wealth—and therefore not be able to enjoy it—the motivation to accumulate more than enough to satisfy short-term desires is weak.[2] It is in this sense that the pattern of borrowing and sharing has its leveling effect: a family experiences an unexpected need; they do not have enough surplus to meet the need and, therefore, they borrow from or share with other families who do have some excess, thus improving their own condition and reducing the minimal surplus of others. At the same time the recipient family establishes an obligation to reciprocate when their condition improves and when their benefactors are in need. This pattern is so well established that an Indian in the Agency office laughed to the Superintendent about government support of Indians. He said it would be impossible for an Indian to starve because of a minimum below which others will not allow him to go.

Within each of the Island villages one family or household sometimes tends to emerge that is conspicuously more acculturated than the others. This household tends to be *future oriented*. Of necessity, to reach this position they restrict important social relations with other families in the community. They do not involve themselves in the borrowing and sharing pattern to the same extent as others, although even they cannot go below a minimum of sharing without severing all relations. Not infrequently these families are in a position of formal authority, such as chief councillor. They have the most material wealth and they tend to plan for the future which often includes plans for leaving the village. Subsisting oriented villagers control the behavior of others by rewarding, among other things, conformity to their norm of not-rising-too-high (not becoming over-acculturated to White middle-class standards). Reward comes in the form of continued, close social interaction with other members of the village. Individuals who attempt to rise too high suffer deprivation of positive reinforcements in varying degrees. In some cases this deprivation is not too punishing because alternative villages are available to which they can migrate; but of course by moving they sever themselves from important social and kinship bonds. Many of these Indian families, who are classed as "progressive" by local Whites, are gradually migrating from their home Reserve to larger social and economic centers.

Stanley Philip is significantly acculturated (future oriented). He lives in Alert Bay and admits that he is "neither fish nor fowl in the Indian world." He knows that a large element of hostility and suspicion is directed toward him by other Indians, and to a certain extent by Whites. Stanley is often tempted to cut off all relations with Indians so he can improve his own position, but he is held back because of his desire to help them—even if in ways they do not want to be helped. On the other hand, members of the village sometimes make disparaging remarks about him for not doing anything for them. One reason for their criticism of him, however, is not so much that he has not done anything for them, but that in being more future oriented and in attaining a certain amount of material success he has had to violate many of the behavior standards held by the subsisting oriented members of the village.

Reciprocity and "non-stinginess" are two important norms guiding inter-

---

[2] This is, of course, only one of the reasons why an acquisitive tendency among the subsisting oriented class is low.

personal relations among the members of the subsisting oriented class. Both are related to the people's expectations of sharing and borrowing. Individuals who want to maintain their position within the network of social relations must reciprocate and be generous. A person who drinks someone else's beer on one occasion must furnish the beer on another, and an individual who buys beer but is stingy with it, that is, closely controls its consumption or removes the supply, is open to criticism. John Patch, for example, bought beer at Echo Bay and returned to the village with six of us. He drank the beer that was offered to him on the way back and then took his own beer to Paul Moon's house. He is reputed to have taken one case which did not belong to him. Frank Bean criticized John saying, "He drinks other people's beer, but won't share his own!" At another time Simon Cedar drank with a group in Alert Bay. At closing time he bought beer along with several others and took it away to drink by himself or with another group. Later he returned to the original party and was forcibly asked to leave. It was explained to me that, "It's not fair to drink all your own beer and then try to get in on the other party."

Sometimes norms of generosity and reciprocity come into conflict with other norms such as the generalized dislike of party crashers. Throughout the evening of a party to which I was invited, different people came to the door and asked to be let in. All of them were refused. The doors and windows were locked. A persistent couple, Daniel and Vera Drake, were alternately ignored in their attempts to come in and told to go away. Vera did most of the talking through the locked door, calling for both Patrick Cedar and Norma Rochelle to let them in. Finally Vera got mad and gave up when she and Daniel had been ignored or told to go away half a dozen times. She called to Pat, "All right, you just remember this the next time you come to my house for food." Pat is a bachelor who frequently eats with them and is dependent upon them for many favors. With the above comment the Drakes stalked away. Pat and his sister Norma jumped up and called for them to come back. They did not. Norma closed the door and said, for lack of anything better, "There's nobody there." Both Pat and Norma were disturbed for a few minutes. As the party progressed and those attending became more inebriated, the comments made to potential party crashers became ruder.

Noninterference, that is, the norm of not becoming involved in troublesome events unless they specifically concern the individual, is one of the strongest standards regulating interpersonal behavior within the village. We realized the power of non-interference on our return to Gilford from the Christmas holidays. Ordinarily, whenever we left the village, our return was heralded by children and adults who came down to the float when they saw our boat or plane come in. When we returned after Christmas, there was no one on the float. As we trudged up the path to the school, Edna, one of the village councillors, met us. She asked if we had stopped in Alert Bay. When we said no, she said, "Then you don't know what's happened," and explained how sorry she was that someone had broken into the school. "This never happened here before," Edna said, adding that she had no idea who had done it. We entered the teacherage to find a broken living room window boarded up by one of the villagers. There were blotches of dried blood here and there among the pieces of broken glass and it was evident from the location of bloody thumb prints that the thief had unsuccessfully searched for liquor. He had taken many of my wife's clothes, pieces of underwear and toiletries, all of which suggested that the thief was Benny, a villager with transvestite tendencies.

I approached Benny and invited him to our quarters to have a talk and to have tea. He knew he had stolen articles from the teacherage, but because he had been drunk at the time he said he could not remember where the things were now. We told him we would not press charges or give his name to the Indian Agent if he returned the things he stole. Benny went from house to house pleading for knowledge of the stolen garments. Each person he asked referred him to someone else who *might* know. He finally talked to a man who admitted he *might* know where they were, and the two men went together to look. The objects were lying in a loose bundle at the bottom of a bluff on the beach. A few days earlier a man had seen them and commented on their location to others, among whom was the man who admitted tentative knowledge of their presence. Probably most people in the village knew where they were, but they were unwilling to admit to any knowledge. They were unwilling to interfere in a problem which did not specifically concern them. A number of people later said to me that they had been afraid of becoming involved.

At times, in every society, people must make a choice between conflicting norms. For example, the norm of noninterference is often overridden when a close kin such as a child, sibling or spouse is being beaten by someone of more distant kin affiliation or by a non-kinsman. Joe Abel, for example, started to rough up his sister. Charles Bean took his mother's side against Joe, his uncle; Joe's son, Andy, sided with his father by throwing beer on Charles. Joe tried to break up the resulting fight between Andy and Charles, and another man jumped onto Joe's neck. Ultimately Joe's arm and several other parts of his body were burned when Charles pushed him against the stove. One eye was badly blackened, and he broke an ankle. On other occasions interpersonal alliances involving some of the same people take quite different forms, although certain people typically ally themselves with one another unless they themselves are fighting. Although alliances tend to be based on both kinship ties and bonds of friendship, individuals must at times also choose between loyalties of friendship and kinship.

Conflict is a prominent feature of interpersonal relations within individual households and within the village at large. In fact, conflict may be viewed as part of normal social interaction within the community, but it is rarely of such magnitude that it seriously disrupts the order and stability of the system. Indian families at Gilford and throughout the area are characterized both by their flexibility and by their extensibility. Friends and relatives move in with a family for greater or lesser periods of time, sometimes permanently. Patrick's household provides an illustration. Pat lives with his sister, Norma, his sister's common-law husband, and their three children. Open conflict exists between Patrick and his sister. Even though the house formally belongs to Pat, he complains that Norma tries to dominate the household. She sometimes attacks him verbally as well as physically, and once she slashed him with a broken beer bottle. The relationship between Patrick and his brother-in-law, Henry, is frequently discordant as well. At one time

Patrick borrowed Henry's speedboat and Henry later accused him of damaging it and threatened to take him to court unless he made reparations. Patrick retaliated, "Oh yeah, how about the rent you've never paid me?"

Rarely are outsiders such as the Royal Canadian Mounted Police brought into family conflicts because each disputant has an expansible set of complaints against the other. For every complaint made by one person, the second may retaliate with another on which the former may, in turn, draw up new ones. Because of this mutual set of grievances, a sense of justice is violated to have one person press charges against the second. Threats of such action are frequent, but such threats are rarely acted upon. Mutual complaints tend to reinforce conflict and future complaints, thus perpetuating them.

Whereas public displays of affection between spouses are unusual among the members of the village and among the Indians in the Gilford area generally, public displays of marital discord are not infrequent. The discrepancy between the two sometimes leads casual observers to the conclusion that Indian marriages are strife-ridden, but this is not generally true. An incident of obvious affection between spouses, for example, occurred when Ambrose Cedar fell asleep on one of the bunks in his boat. Louisa, his common-law wife, was very concerned about him because of his bad heart, and she insisted that he not be awakened. At one point while he was sleeping she moved across the boat to his side and put her face very gently against his, ran her hands through his hair and kissed his cheeks and forehead. She held him for several minutes. Later in the evening after we moved to Ambrose's place, he fondly patted her a few times.

Physical and verbal aggression between husband and wife is common, but most typically occurs during or following periods of drinking. Wife beatings occur periodically along with other forms of physical aggression. One husband has beaten his wife several times including while she was pregnant and, as a consequence, she aborted and has not been able to have any children. Beaten wives sometimes move out of their homes and live for a period of time with another family within the village, but more often they move away from the village altogether. Some wives say that they wait for their husbands "to get drunk and pass out" and then take revenge. Verbal conflict is more typical among some of the villagers than physical aggression, especially during periods of sobriety. To illustrate, Herbert took one of his young sons to the store at Simoom Sound and stopped at the beer parlor on the way back. While we were there the boy slipped off a log and fell partially into the water. A second man who was leaving the beer parlor saw the incident and commented on it to Herb's wife when he returned to the village. When we returned home late in the evening, Gertie met us at the float. She angrily called Herb a bastard and asked, "What kind of a fucking father are you anyway, keeping your son out this late?" She refused to speak to him except angrily for several days.

Jealousy is the most common cause of aggression between spouses. If an individual learns that his spouse has been involved in an illicit affair he may severely chastise his partner, physically and verbally. Marital jealousy is very common, and on one occasion Harold Dick sat outside his house most of the day because his common-law wife was angry with him. "She's jealous because she saw me with a woman in the Bay." Herbert also confided that he used to be very jealous of Gertie, but "I started thinking about it last summer and decided that if a woman loves me, fine; and if she doesn't there's nothing I can do about it anyway."

The preference or ideal among members of the community calls for sexual fidelity in marriage, but extramarital relations are not at all uncommon. Quite often in the past—but sometimes today too—an intermediary was used to make arrangements for an amour. As described to me by an elderly villager, a man or woman who was attracted to another sent a third person with a note saying, in effect, "I have liked you for a long time and would like to know if you would be interested in sharing my bed with me." If the second person was interested, he might respond, "I have liked you very much from the first time I saw you, and my thoughts have been constantly about you. I would be pleased to accept your invitation." The next step was to make more specific arrangements regarding time and place. In order to avoid shaming the uninvolved spouses, attempts were made by the lovers, as well as by members of the community, to keep the news from them. Husbands often beat their wives when they discovered what was happening. According to the same man, divorce was not formalized; one simply left his spouse and publicly, informally disclaimed her.[3] Either person might then remarry. Today marriages are still elastic and do not break up because of occasional infidelity, although repetitive unfaithfulness creates a great strain in the marriage relation and is instrumental in fracturing some. Some people say it is unusual for women to remain sexually faithful to their husbands if they are absent for a long period of time. Women who are obvious about their sexual activities, however, are sometimes contemptuously called pigs. Villagers almost always use discretion in the act of sexual intercourse, whether it be between husband and wife or illicitly. Spouses usually wait until other members of the household are asleep, but during times of drinking discretionary bars are somewhat lowered. The morning following a party or during the party itself a man and a woman— married or not—may be found, as the villagers say, on a bed "passed out together."

Conflict within the village sometimes gives the impression of being rampant, but effective social controls are nonetheless operating. Serious damage to the body or to property is rarely committed even during periods of the most unrestrained parties and fighting. Windows or furniture may be broken, but houses are not burned; a person may have his nose broken or his face cut with glass, but he is not mortally stabbed. In fact, according to the RCMP, major crimes of all types are infrequent among Indians. Most problems among Whites and Indians are minor offenses against body or property and are associated with drinking; when serious offenses occur, however, they are usually committed by Whites. Crimes committed by Indians are usually not premeditated. One RCMP officer reported, for example, that an Indian may see a power saw lying unattended outside and will pick it up. When challenged, the individual who committed the theft often readily admits having taken it and hiding it under his bed.

[3] This was probably not true, at least for ranking members of the community, during the famous Potlatch period, aspects of which are described in Chapter 5.

We are inclined to think that this last statement, however, is something of an overstatement.

The valued behavior standards on which the members of the community operate are not always clear to us, but the major forms of social control that are applied when norms are violated are more easily recognized. Among the Kwakiutl the process of interpersonal interaction itself is one of the most powerful mechanisms of social control. As we said above, a sense of security and, not insignificantly, identity among the subsisting oriented group is firmly anchored within the community. Because of it, special or coercive control devices are not usually needed. In the first place through a long socialization period individuals have internalized most of the normative standards in such a way that they are able to evaluate the behavior of others and to agree that a norm has been violated, and the offender is aware of the legitimacy of the evaluation against him. For most members of the village the community has become the primary reference group, that is, the group with which they identify themselves and in relation to which they think about themselves. Through this reference group an individual establishes his frames of reference through which perceptions, experiences and ideas about himself are ordered. To this extent members of the village are in a position to give positive social rewards and punitive sanctions. Any threat to one's position within this system—such as the withdrawal of acceptance, favorable recognition or approval—poses a personal threat to the individual. Thus, the withdrawal of favorable recognition and approval, in threat or in fact, is a powerful social control mechanism. It is often communicated to the individual through such media as gossip, indirect criticism and constrained social relations. This interpretation receives strong support from Pat Cedar, who had been drinking and felt free to discuss his feelings about members of the community and his relationship to them. He expressed his feelings of dependency on the affection and positive support he receives from some close kinsmen in the village. Throughout the conversation he cited specific situations where love was given to and withheld from him by these people.

Control is also effected through the pattern of ignoring someone. If invitations are being made for a party and the host does not want one person in the group to attend, he ignores that person, behaving as if he were not there; he neither looks at nor talks to the shunned person. The other invited guests behave in the same way. This technique is also used on other occasions to avoid trouble with an individual who is trying to incite a quarrel or fight. These social control techniques are not as effective, of course, among individuals who do not normally live in the village and who have little emotional or social investment within it. Higher authority is sometimes invoked when outsiders create or threaten to create trouble. Threats may be made to call the RCMP, or the authority of the Band council may be used in forcing the person out of the village. This type of control has a double edge. On the one hand it controls the behavior of outsiders, but on the other hand it generates an attitude of limited involvement on the part of visitors so that they never reach the point of being effectively controlled by the more subtle methods of social control normally employed.

Drinking and Social Interaction

The use and sharing of intoxicants have important relevance to subsisting and future oriented groups, and through the use of alcohol many of the community's normative standards and social control mechanisms are projected into bold relief. Some future oriented Indians do not drink, and those who do, seldom drink with other members of the village at parties. Several reasons for this are apparent. Individuals in the future oriented class would soon be depleted of their accumulated material goods if they drank with and shared their liquor with others in the normal manner, since the typical drinking pattern among the subsisting oriented group is one of drinking until one's money is exhausted. By not participating in drinking parties, members of the future oriented group are exposed to sharp criticisms by subsisting oriented Indians. One member of the future oriented category (Victor Philip, the previous chief councillor) occasionally drinks with his family and accepts a bottle or two of beer from others, but he does not join any major drinking parties. Victor claims not to drink for his children's sake, saying it is foolish for parents to talk against drinking and then to drink in front of their children. A further indication of the difference in attitude between the two groups is demonstrated by Benny Otter's comment to me. Acting on his authority as chief councillor, Victor refused to recommend Benny for relief. Victor lectured Benny about drinking away all his money. He pointed out how he had saved enough money in the fishing season to support his family during the winter, and told Benny that he should have done the same rather than squander it on liquor. Benny replied, "You're privileged that you don't drink"; he continued his story to me with an explanation of the enjoyment he receives from drinking parties. During the summer of 1962, Benny made about $3100, spent $200 on beer, paid a fish company for a new net, net repairs and other expenses, and ended the season with a gain of $37. This is not unusual.

Chief Philip, also a non-drinking member of the future oriented category, has strong feelings about drinking. Although he was one of the people who fought for the privilege of Indians to drink in the same manner as other Canadian citizens, Stanley now wonders if he were wise in doing so. He contends that Indians learned to drink heavily and rapidly by imitating local White loggers and fishermen. He would like to see Indians drink in moderation, but he doubts that they ever will because they have never been exposed to this style of drinking.

Drinking is the most popular and frequent pastime activity in the village. An informal, minimal count that I maintained of the incidence of drinking in the village while we were at Gilford yields an average of six days per month. This figure relates to periods during which a few families or most of the village were drinking, and they include periods from one day to six days of more or less continuous drinking. Sequential days of drinking do not necessarily imply that the same people are involved throughout, but indicate, as one villager insightfully pointed out, that when one group begins drinking others want to as well. The more who drink the more who want to drink until most of the village is involved and a plateau is reached. The people who begin drinking when the episode begins are often not the ones who are drinking when it is completed, unless enough time has elapsed for them to quit, become somewhat rested, and begin again. Typically, however, drinking episodes last for only one or two days.

The personal goal of drinking is to get drunk or to drink until one "passes out" or falls asleep. Once a person begins to drink we noted a sense of urgency on his part to continue until he is totally inebriated. While part of this style of drinking may be related to imitative behavior, it also seems related to the fact that drinking on other than licensed premises was illegal before 1962. Despite the fact that it was unlawful, Indians drank within the village and on their boats when they had access to liquor from bootlegging Whites. They tended to drink as much as they could as quickly as they could, thereby minimizing the risk of being caught because they threw the empty bottles overboard—or discarded the full bottles if it became necessary.

Drinking is now fully legal for the Indians. One of the village men remarked on the role played by bootleggers in the past. The conversation dealt with the time when Indians were dependent on Whites for acquiring intoxicants, and the village man quipped, "Back in the days when Whites were *useful* . . ." The gibe elicited a mirthful response from everyone on the boat, including the two Whites who had earlier been sources of liquor for most of the men at the party.

No one leaves a gathering until all the alcohol has been consumed, and the amount of available liquor contributes to the definition of a successful party. Men often spend everything they have, including money that was intended for food or other necessities. If one wants more beer he might crash somebody else's party or steal beer from an ongoing party. Jeffrey and Alice Hardy, for example, were having a party in their house along with two other people. Earlier that day the four of them had picked up six bottles of whiskey and eleven cases of beer. A group from one of the other parties within the village knew about this store of liquor and unsuccessfully attempted to crash Jeffrey's party. Benny, one of the members of this group, returned later and knocked out one of Jeffrey's windows in his attempt to get in. Jeffrey told Benny to go home; he had his own house and bed. "I don't bother you when you're drinking. Don't bother me!" He nailed his windows closed, but Benny made a second abortive attempt to get in by shattering a window in Jeffrey's door. Later that night, sometime after Jeffrey and Alice had gone to bed, Benny did manage to get into the house and was caught rifling through the suitcase under the bed where Alice hides her belongings. Jeffrey sent him home again, but he believes Benny was somehow able to steal four bottles of his whiskey because it was reported the next day that an empty whiskey bottle was seen in Benny's house; Jeffrey was the only person in the village who had hard liquor. On another occasion Norma Rochelle reports that she had six cases of beer in her house during a party, but the following morning only two cases of empties were left—four full cases had disappeared during the party.

Liquor may be obtained through ready cash, through stealing from a party, through crashing a party or through pawning one's personal or stolen possessions. Men who carve or paint sell their work at a great reduction in price, and some Whites in the area are pleased to do business under these circumstances. Many old and valuable ceremonial masks and other artifacts are sold for a fraction of their real worth to Whites because the latter know they can name their price with a minimum of bargaining when Indians are drinking and want money. Indians later accuse Whites of cheating them of their heritage because of these and related types of transactions. Methods used to obtain alcohol, however, are controlled and channeled within strict limits. Physical violence, for example, is almost never directed, in threat or in fact, against a licensed vendor who refuses to serve an individual when his supply of cash is gone.

Gilford Islanders are noted for their heavy drinking. This is due in part to the fact that few villages among the Islanders have such easy access to a source of beer. Despite the relative intensification of drinking at Gilford and the consequent fights and other disruptive incidents, the RCMP say they have less trouble with this village than most of the others. The reasons why Gilford people create less police trouble than many of the other villages are not entirely clear except that they appear to have fewer feuds than other outlying villages and their social control mechanisms are fairly effective.

Gilford Island Kwakiutl are not only thought of by others as heavy drinkers, but they think of themselves as hardy drinkers. This was expressed to us by Vera Drake in the following way: "Us Indians are tough! We can stay up all night and drink, and sleep the next day." Occasionally some of the villagers become concerned about drinking too much, however. Cecelia Cedar confided in my wife that she is beginning to like the taste of beer—really like it—and finds it hard to stay away from it. She and her husband do not fight except when they are drinking, or at least not much, and Cecelia feels she is bordering on or may become a drunkard, although she did not use these words.[4] Evelyn asked if she likes the beer itself or the effect it has on her, and she answered that she likes the beer.

One of the positive functions of drinking for the Gilford Islanders is to help relax normally constricted interpersonal communication, thus allowing dissatisfactions to be freely and openly expressed in ways they would not be if the person were entirely sober. Expressions of discontent tend to be circuitous and masked in normal, day-to-day interaction. It is an exceptional encounter for one person to be directly confronted by a second on some unpleasant matter. More typically, a disaffected person talks about someone else with the hope that the information will get back to the second person. Edgar Drake, manager of the village soccer team, for example, wanted to resign. Rather than tell the team about his decision, he simply did not show up for any of the scheduled meetings and, as a result, they were cancelled. Even though Edgar and Joe Abel, president of the club, saw each other daily, Edgar never told Joe he wanted to quit. He told a friend who told Joe, and then Joe told the others, "I *hear* Edgar's going to quit."

On another occasion, four white men from Echo Bay approached us with the idea of joining together the parent-teacher groups from Gilford and from Echo Bay. We brought up their proposal at the next village meeting. None of the villagers said anything until Herbert, who had been drinking, suggested that the

---

[4] The incidence of alcoholism among the Kwakiutl is reported to be very low. We know of no Kwakiutl, in fact, who can be correctly diagnosed as an alcoholic.

Echo Bay parent-teacher group vote first about the amalgamation—before the villagers commit themselves. "They might say no and make us go hang-dog around those White men." His suggestion was well received, and several people remarked after the meeting how happy they were that Herb had been drinking; otherwise the suggestion would not have been made. The two groups were not amalgamated.

Drinking not only improves the effectiveness of interpersonal communication, but it also lowers inhibitions regarding sex. Sweet, red wine, which is consumed as rapidly as beer, is considered to be an aphrodisiac for women. Frank Bean told me that women should not drink wine because it excites them; "it makes them feel loving and want to go to bed with a man." One night Willis Drake had been drinking wine when he knocked on Henry Rochelle's door and asked to be let in. Henry wanted his wife to ignore it, but she got up and let him in. Willis, who had the wives of two other men with him, asked for some whiskey to go with their wine. Norma poured them each a glass and went back to bed. One wife left soon after that. The next morning Willis and Mary Bean, the other wife, were in bed together, "passed out." Harold Dick is particularly noted for his sexual activities when he drinks. As the Kwakiutl express it, "he tries to fool around" with the daughters of his common-law wife. Once he placed a gas-soaked rag over the nose of one girl to "make her sleep more soundly, and tried to play with her." She woke up and scared him away. On another occasion Harold was caught "playing" with a two and one-half year old girl. The mother was outraged and said that she was going to report him to the RCMP the following week, which she did not do. Daniel Drake dislikes his stepfather for these sexual advances on his sisters and other girls; and when he is drinking, Dan often attacks Harold.

Villagers are physically modest on most occasions, but through the reduction of inhibitory mechanisms while drinking they become less so. On one occasion Larry's wife, Cecilia, came on deck from the gill-net cabin to urinate. She whispered to Patrick, who was on deck with me, and Patrick explained that I should go below for a moment. Cecilia said, "I'm not shy in front of Larry and Patrick, but you're. . . ." The sentence trailed off, probably to be completed as "a White man. You're different from us and might not understand." On the trip back from Echo Bay, everyone was sitting below deck drinking beer. Cecilia sat next to Frank Bean. Frank excused himself to go on deck and, as he got up, Larry yelled at Cecilia, "Get your hand off his prick." If he had not been drinking, he would not have been so outspoken.

Latent hostility is directly expressed (often through fights) during periods of drinking, and tensions that might otherwise fester and lead to less manageable strains are not infrequently resolved. As expressed by one of our informants, people usually realize that it is through the influence of alcohol that they fight in the first place. Fights may occur among a number of people, among all ages and across sexes. A man in his fifties can fight with a teenager on an equal basis. Fights are almost always contextualized in periods of drinking, but grudges are usually not carried on into sober periods. A middle-aged man at Village Island, for example, kicked his elderly mother and broke her hip. She was taken to the hospital and was later shocked to learn that the RCMP had sentenced her son to prison because he beat her. News of the affair spread rapidly throughout the area and public reaction to it gives an indication of the normative structure involved; many people were indignant at the man for his actions, but their ill feelings shifted to the RCMP for interfering.

Even though women drink almost as much as men, they are less physically combative. They too, however, occasionally become involved in fights, and they are certainly as knowledgeable as men in verbal aggression. Two of my journal-note entries reflect these facts.

> Emily was injured on New Year's Eve at Victor's place where they are now living. According to Norman, the place was fairly well torn up: a large mirror was smashed, a new radio ruined, and so forth. Emily somehow got on the bottom of four men in a fight and she was kicked in the stomach and in the back, damaging one of her kidneys. Several other women joined the fight too. Archie and Norm took Edna to the hospital in Alert Bay. The doctors doubt that the kidney will totally heal. After being released from the hospital she had one and one-half bottles of beer and passed out, apparently because of her stomach or kidney injury.

> The most serious trouble occurred at Jeffrey's. For some reason, Edna was in there and Darlene [her daughter] wanted her to come out. Jeffrey told Darlene to leave and she started breaking his windows. Finally he threw Darlene out of the house, violently shoving her against the post on the porch. Ralph [her brother] picked up an empty bucket and threw it at Jeff, striking him in the back.

Fights frequently result in black eyes and swollen lips, but when serious injury occurs, relatively little attention is given to it. Joe, a two-hundred-fifty pounder, walked on his broken foot for a month before he had the doctor place it in a cast. Because of his great weight he found crutches uncomfortable and abandoned them as soon as possible, and he took his cast off before the scheduled time. At another time Brian Abel broke his hand when he and Lawrence Cedar got into a fight on Lawrence's gill-netter. Larry ducked and Brian hit his fist against the engine of the craft. Brian did not seek medical attention for his hand even though it was broken, badly swollen and discolored. Most of the villagers agreed, however, that his behavior was extreme when, the next day, he tried to help the other men scythe down some of the grass and weeds in the village.

A few Kwakiutl tend to "go haywire" when they drink. Going haywire is defined by the villagers as unusual and the term implies an unrestrained, uncontrolled lashing out at other people and things. Lauren went haywire, according to Lawrence, and started shooting off Lawrence's 30–30 at the latter's gill-netter. The next day Lawrence made the comment, "My brother-in-law is really a haywire guy! I won't drink with him again. I didn't enjoy the party last night!" Another incident occurred between Joe and me. One day, after dinner I went to see Joe in order to get my clam fork which he had borrowed. He was eating clam chowder and was almost in a daze from drinking when I entered. He was in a foul mood and had been, I learned later, talking most of the day about fighting and not being afraid of anyone. He glowered silently, not greeting me when I came in.

After finishing his bowl of chowder and ladling out another, he finally asked what I wanted. I explained that I wanted my clam fork. He did not acknowledge my request, but began talking about not liking to be pushed around and "standing up for my own rights, fighting anybody any time." Up to this point his comments were simply a generalized verbal aggression directed at nothing in particular. After a few minutes he began working himself up and slammed the table with his fist. He intended to fight and I was his only accessible target. He menacingly removed his coat, but I told him I had not come to fight with him, that I did not have anything against him and that, in fact, I liked him. This pacified him for only a moment. He started working up to another rage, pounding the table more vehemently and stripped to his tee shirt. It was clear that I could not get up from my place without being attacked, and within a few moments I realized that he was not going to be pacified. I sat there motionlessly because each movement of my hands or head incited him to further rage. During the hour that I was with him, he mumbled in a semi-articulate rage about being councillor in the village but "not giving a God damned hell about any fucking cocksucker in the whole fucking village." Several times he apparently misunderstood what I was saying since he is very hard of hearing, and thought I was insulting him. More than once he picked up the table and acted as if he were going to throw it over me; once he tipped it so forcefully that most of the dishes shattered on the floor and on the bench where I was sitting. Joe's sister and her two daughters were frightened and ran out of the house. Later he picked up a beer bottle which he started to break to use as a weapon against me. Eventually I was able to retreat uninjured. The next day Joe remembered nothing about the incident until his sister and others reminded him of what had happened.

In no sense do drinking episodes always involve aggression, but when fights do occur, they are almost always within the context of drinking. The following description of a party, drawn from my journal notes, suggests the common tenor of village parties, although it contains more disparate elements than many parties. The description reveals obvious as well as subtle forms of aggression, tenderness, rancor, compassion, conflict and cooperation.

> The party was in a state of transition as I walked in. New people were arriving from Edna's and some of those who had been there began to leave. During the evening 15 people came in and stayed, or remained only for a few minutes. Charles was annoyed that people were coming to drink his beer even though they had beer at their own parties. As the party progressed some attempts were made at Indian-singing, but these attempts did not last very long. Alex tried singing some popular songs in English but was soon silenced by Edward. An attempt was made at playing *lahel* (Indian "dice"), but this too was abortive. I was buttonholed by Cecil who talked about mining and prospecting up Kingcome. Later I was buttonholed by Charles and by Norman who talked about soccer. Eventually I was able to free myself from these corners and mix and listen to the general tone of the evening. Charles at one point made the comment that he likes to fight. Clarence and Joe were having a running battle-conversation throughout the evening about fighting each other. Clarence made the comment that all he can remember about his childhood is Joe, his father, coming home after drinking and throwing him around like a wet towel. "I learned to fight the hard way." Joe only smiled at this. Early in the evening Joe had asked Clarence to wrestle with him, but the latter declined saying

that the house was not the proper place. Later Clarence tried to pick a fight with his father. He said, "You've had your day, now let me have mine." Each of them said that he could beat the other in a fight if it came to it. Charles had skinned knuckles from a wrestling match outside with Cecil. Charles praised Cecil's strength but said that he, Charles, was faster. It is common for one man to praise the ability or strength of another.

Alex and Darlene sat on the couch for part of the evening talking. Someone started to tease them and they protested that they were only "best friends." The women tended to talk among themselves as did the men, but there was no major separation by sex; each intermingled with the other. Peter and Greg sat on the floor not saying anything. Both were quite drunk, especially Peter who sat quietly with an owlish expression on his face. There was no consistency of seating among the people; they moved around at will, depending on interest and availability of seating. A number of people came in and out of the house on different occasions. Probably no one sat there for the entire evening without going out at least once.

Ralph came in once and said that Fred was stabbing himself in the stomach. Fred and Ruby had had a fight at Edna's. Ed went out as did one or two others. Charles suggested that Greg go too, but the latter declined as did some others (exemplifying the pattern of noninterference and noninvolvement). They returned in about half an hour saying that Fred was all right, and sleeping now. I did not discover whether he really did stab himself. Edna was sitting there at the time but did not go out to see what the problem was. She left it up to the men, even though Fred and Ruby (her daughter) were living at her place. Because Fred and Ruby have been living together for about one year their (common-law) union tends to be accepted by most people.

During part of the evening Alex and Ed sat on the couch side by side. Edward had his arm around Alex's shoulders and Alex was holding that hand, playing with the fingers. I have been struck several times by the importance of physical aggression among the men and the natural warmth of physical contact on certain occasions which contrasts with or is the obverse of such aggression. There is no shame or embarrassment in such an expression of friendship.

Some of the kids, for example, Ralph (age 13) and Willie (age 10) were up most of the night. Ralph had a bottle of whiskey in his pocket which was apparently given to him to hold in trust for someone. I later heard that someone was giving Ralph beer. A great deal of drinking is going on in the village tonight. Lawrence went to the Bay this morning and returned this evening with some beer. Cecilia (his wife) called a plane to pick her up, but by the time it got here she decided not to go because she was afraid that Larry would be on his way back to the village. This is the end of a clam tide and most people have some extra money to spend. More drinking is going on now than since before Christmas.

Death and Religion

Accidents are the principal cause of death among the Kwakiutl and drowning is the greatest single form of accidental death. Drowning often occurs in contexts of drinking when, for example, a man gets drunk in the Bay, buys more beer and attempts to travel back to his home village. We suspect that some reputedly accidental drownings are not accidents at all. They are probably suicides. The true incidence of suicide among the Kwakiutl is unknown, but threats and attempts are not unusual and often appear in association with drinking. James Jack, a visitor from another village, was drinking and began talking about death. He recounted an episode when Jennie Drake fell overboard and because of her great weight he could not drag her back onto the gill-netter. She pleaded with him, "If you can't get me up, let me go! Let me go!" With the help of seven men she was brought safely on board, but she wanted to jump back in once rescued. James concluded, "I guess she thought she should have died." He then summarized what may be a common Kwakiutl acceptance of death. "We never know when or where. Each minute we live is just one more of life. We never know what tomorrow will bring." He talked about natural death in the hospital and accidental death from such causes as drowning. I asked him which was a better way of dying and he responded indirectly by say that his father had been drowned as had his father's father and so would he, probably. Continuing, he said that his half-brother probably wanted to die at the time of his drowning. The latter had "fallen" overboard five times shortly prior to the final incident.

Funeral services follow procedures legislated by the various religious denominations. Church services, however, are often supplemented by more traditional practices to help kinsmen "forget their tears." An important chief of the Tsawatenok tribe died in March, 1963. The services for him were longer and more elaborate than most, but the range of events is similar for individuals of lesser importance. As I recorded in my field notes:

Monday Night

A church service was called by some of the W.A. [Anglican Women's Auxiliary] women in the evening. The Anglican Lay Reader did not know about it until it was over: About eighty people attended the service which was held in the community hall at Kingcome. It lasted from 8:30 to 10:30 and was conducted in Kwakwala. Refreshments of coffee, cakes, cookies and graham crackers were served at the end of the service. The service progressed in the following order: one song was sung from the Kwakwala hymnal and then someone by arrangement was asked to come to the front of the hall and talk. Most of the people talked about the deceased man and the impact of his death on his family. They thanked everyone for attending the service. Chiefs from other villages were the major spokesmen, but the service was officiated by the chief councillor from Kingcome. Songs were led by an elderly woman and the laywoman from Gilford was asked to give the concluding prayer.

Tuesday Afternoon

The official Anglican service began at 2:00 P.M. in the church. There were about 130 people in attendance. The service followed the standard Anglican form for a funeral service and lasted about half an hour. Six pallbearers carried the grey, commercial coffin to the graveyard half a mile from the village where the service was continued. About 50 people were at the grave which had been dug previously by some of the younger members of the deceased's family—sons and close relatives. The Lay Reader made a graveside reading and left; two other people stepped to the head of the grave and spoke briefly in Kwakwala. Much of the time at the grave was silent and very somber; some of the members of the deceased's family cried, especially his wife, daughter and son. The older son said in a loud, clear voice, nodding his head in finality, "*Hala kesla, ump; hala kesla,*" "good-bye, father; good-bye." During this time the pallbearers had been taking turns filling the grave. Two songs initiated in Kwakwala from the hymnal began weakly but picked up force as more mourners joined in. People began returning to the village, and about fifteen remained when the grave was completely covered and the artificial flower wreaths were placed on the mound. An old, ragged piece of lumber was stuck in the grave to mark the head.

Funeral Service: Indian

Following the graveyard service people went to the big-house, *gyux*, and continued the funeral service in Kwakwala and in Indian style. The big-house has an earthen floor, carved poles at either end and a cedar-shake roof. A huge opening in the roof allows the fire and smoke to escape. About 100 people attended in the *gyux*. A large, blazing fire about five feet across and three feet high was placed in the middle of the earthen floor. Twelve men were seated at the end of the hall on either side of the log drum. One of the men had a snare drum on which an Indian design was painted. Four Indian funeral songs were sung at the beginning, and a speech was delivered about the potlatches which the deceased had given during his lifetime. Other speakers mentioned similar topics. The deceased's oldest son, dressed as a hamatsa [cannibal dancer], entered the dance area through a curtained entrance; he passed completely through the building and out the main entrance. He will dance again tonight at the potlatch at which time his mother will give him some Indian names which belonged to his father.

Four women sitting at the head of the *gyux* near the rhythm section were dressed in button blankets. They had been especially asked to honor the deceased. A man from Gilford passed by, placing eagle-down on their heads. He circled the room making a ring of down on the floor behind him. This portion of the funeral ceremony lasted until 5:00 P.M., at which time it was adjourned until 7:00 P.M. the same evening.

Commemorative Potlatch and Indian Dances

The ceremony reconvened at 7:00 P.M. in the *gyux*. About 200–250 people attended; no empty seats or spaces were available, consequently many people had to stand around the door and outside. The building was filled with smoke much of the evening except when dry logs were placed on the fire, which created a good draft through the ceiling. At one time during the evening the roof caught fire but was quickly extinguished with several buckets of water from above. This potlatch followed the same general format as the one at Turnour earlier this year [see Chapter 5]. The same class of dances was performed at Turnour, but the specific dances varied in form and content because people at Kingcome have the legitimate right to perform certain dances and not others. Six masked dances were performed during the evening, including one *qolus*, "Thunderbird," and one Mountain Goat Hunter which differed from that at Turnour. A man costumed as a dog participated with the Hunter. Other features varied as well. There were also several Ermine dancers with their ermine cloaks and masks. Most of the dances, however, were *hamatsa*, the dancers wearing cedar rings around the shoulders and one on the head. Many button blankets are worn during the dances, especially by the women.

The dances lasted until approximately 10:30 P.M. and were followed by the distribution of goods and money. About $250 were distributed by members of the deceased's family. Goods consisted of such things as hand towels, embroidered dish towels, and embroidered pillow cases. Each person appeared to receive two items. About sixty loaves of bread were used for making sandwiches, some of which were made from oulachon. One of the women told me later that the plot had been made to give oulachon sandwiches to Whites to see how they would react. The general consensus among Indians is that Whites do not like oulachon grease or the fish. Coffee, tea, cakes, cookies and cupcakes were also served.

A man from Turnour continued the potlatch for his own purposes after the family of the deceased gave theirs. I could not tell when one ended and the other began except for a verbal comment made in Kwakwala. The same is true of the dances. Each man putting on dances asks different people to dance for him. The latter are then given gifts for performing. During the dances different men occasionally stood up and talked as they did at Turnour. The potlatches and dances today are greatly abbreviated forms of what they once were. Some dances which traditionally took several hours or longer to perform are now performed in a few minutes. Most dances now last only two to four minutes—enough time to circle the fire at least twice in most cases.

Religious beliefs among the villagers range from a firm commitment to the doctrine of a particular church, to a nondoctrinal belief in God and the divinity of Christ, to skepticism or questioning of both and finally to outright disbelief. According to Hilda, the Pentecostal laywoman in the village, most Kwakiutl have religious feelings, but one would have trouble in getting them to express these feelings. At another time she admitted, "Just because they come to church is no sign they profess religion." Not uncommonly someone may say he rarely prays and that, in fact, he does not really think about religion very often. Norman Philip expressed his feelings to me in the following way: "I never get on my hands and knees and pray. Sure, I go sometimes to Hilda's services, but I don't pay much attention to that." Cecil Abel observed, "I'm a materialist, I believe what my hands can touch." Religious feelings vary in intensity at different times. This is reflected in a letter written to us by Hilda in 1964. "Benjamin [Otter] really desires to follow the Lord and reads his Bible and comes to services more, etc. Others have requested special prayer, as they know they are away from the Lord." Benjamin attended services only infrequently while we lived in the village, and at that time he claimed not to be concerned with religion. Most of the members of the community attend the regularly scheduled Pentecostal services in the village at least occasionally. In addition, they often attend the special Anglican and other services that are held within the village from time to time, regardless of the denomination. To this extent villagers may be characterized as being eclectic in religious beliefs. Some frankly admit that they attend church services because others go and because they do not have anything else to do. Church services for some are simply social occasions, but for others they have deeper religious meaning.

Pentecostals do not believe in drinking, smoking, dancing, attending commercial movies, playing cards or the use of facial cosmetics. Because of these restrictions, especially on drinking, it is doubtful that many Indians will become true converts to the church, even though many find it attractive for other reasons.

Hilda supports several church-related activities within the village. She identifies herself as a children's worker and holds Bible Club, Young People's Meetings, and Sunday school once each week. The Bible Club meets after school for about an hour and is designed largely for children from three to twelve years of age. The Young People's Meetings are held during the evening and are restricted to children ten years old and over. They have Bible drills, quizzes, usually a Bible story and sometimes refreshments. Sunday school is held Sunday mornings for all the children. She also holds Sunday evening church services in her house or other village homes for the adults. Special services are held on such occasions as the birth of a baby, a birthday celebration, or a death. Refreshments consisting of sandwiches, cake, cupcakes, Freshie (a flavored powder like Kool-Aid which is mixed with water) and coffee are served following these special services. Food is supplied by the family for whom the special service is being held and is passed around by several adults or teenagers, male or female, while the others remain seated. As in potlatches, one does not customarily refuse food that is offered—even if it is far more than he can eat. The excess is taken home in a paper bag that is often distributed just for that purpose.

Occasionally Pentecostal visitors come to the village and hold services. A White preacher who lives at Turnour plans weekly visits by boat to New Van, Village and Gilford, but because of weather conditions he cannot always make it. Typically church services within the village conform to a standard format: several songs are sung from the hymnal which has been translated into Kwakwala; a prayer is led, usually by one of the villagers in Kwakwala, but sometimes by the deaconess in English; more songs are sung in Kwakwala; a second prayer is made; another song is sung from the hymnal and a collection is made; a passage from the Bible is read or a sermon is delivered if there is a guest speaker; a final song is sung and the service is concluded. The sequence of events is not always as given, but the specific elements are generally included. The villagers, who actively participate in most services, lead prayers, read from the Bible and call requests for hymns to be sung while Hilda plays her accordion. Even though they look at the hymnals as if reading them, most people know the hymns well enough not to be dependent on the translations.

Religious activities continue during the summer months through the Marine Medical Mission Vacation Bible School, which is basically a fundamentalist organization drawing from several denominations. Young adults, usually two young women, live in the village for about three weeks each summer, conducting Bible classes and other church-related activities. They concentrate primarily on children, but they also hold services for adults. The program is designed to be non-denominational in doctrine and is guided by a schedule printed at mission headquarters. The girls work about five hours each day, three hours in the morning with children from age three to twelve, and two hours in the afternoon or evening with the older children.

The daily program begins about 9:30 A.M. when all the children salute the Canadian and church flags, recite the accompanying verse, sing and read from the Bible. Children from age eight to twelve recite their memory verses and listen to a Bible story. The children play organized games outside during their recess. Following this, they work assignments in their workbooks and work on handicrafts such as coloring or cutting figures for flannel board stories. Before leaving, the children are told a story that has a moral and sing some hymns. The activities of the older group are similar to those of the younger, but their schedule is geared to their age level. Occasionally older children play softball or some other organized game in the evening and they may have refreshments following this.

Anglican church services are held infrequently among the Islanders, except at Kingcome where a church has been established for many years and where a lay reader resides. Anglican clergymen are scheduled to visit the Island villages about once a month, but while we were at Gilford services were held once every two to four months. Visits are made on the *Columbia*, which acquired a full-time minister after we left the village. Consequently, services are now reported to be held more frequently.

Competitiveness and mild conflict characterize the relationship between the Pentecostal deaconess and the Anglican lay reader and clergy. According to a minister in the United Church in Alert Bay, Anglicans dislike Pentecostals because the latter encroach on formally allocated Anglican territory. Anglicans and the United Church work fairly well together because each restricts its activities to territories which overlap very little; as a result they do not interfere with and antagonize one another. Hilda was once told by a former Anglican minister at Kingcome, "You're in my territory and therefore under my jurisdiction." She paid no attention to this pronouncement, although she admits that, "This is Anglican territory as far as [church] allotment goes." She says that she attends Anglican services when they are held in the village and sometimes tries to elaborate on a theme which is initiated during an Anglican service, but she attended no Anglican services while we were living at Gilford. She once admitted being annoyed when villagers come to her house to borrow benches, tables or dishes to be used in Anglican services. One representative occasion irritated her, for example, when a village man asked to borrow benches. She asked why he wanted them and he was embarrassed to tell her about the Anglican baptismal ceremony which was about to take place. She had not known that the *Columbia* had called in the village and was at that moment tied to the float.

A useful but rough index of the relative influence of and differential attitudes toward each denomination is found in the unique situation where the two groups held services simultaneously within the village. The Pentacostal service was attended by fifteen people, including eight children; twelve people attended the Anglican service, including four children. The majority of the village attended neither service. Some of the men who were fishing did not attend, as is true of a small group who were drinking. I asked Victor Philip which service he would attend, and he responded, "Well, since I have my choice I guess I won't go to either." A further indicator of religious orientation is found in the composition of the three major church groups in Alert Bay—the United Church, Anglican and Pentecostal. The United Church draws almost exclusively from the White population in Alert Bay, the Anglican from both White and Indian, and the Pentecostal largely from the Indian population. None of the churches has a large or consistent attendance from Indians or Whites. Members of the subsisting oriented class appear to attend Pentecostal services more frequently than Anglican, and members of the future oriented class appear to prefer Anglican more often than Pentecostal

Several reasons exist why relatively more villagers attend Pentecostal services than Anglican. An Anglican communion service furnishes an example of the difference between the two. It was attended by sixteen villagers, ten of whom took communion. The service, which lasted thirty minutes, was read from the Book of Common Prayer, and two hymns were sung in English which were notably lacking in spontaneity and volume. Members of the village were somewhat uncomfortable during the service because it was highly formalized and replete with symbolism in dress and paraphernalia. Both of the clergymen who officiated were in their clerical frocks. The members of the village are more accustomed to Pentecostal services with their spontaneity and casualness. The fact that a considerable part of the Pentacostal services are in Kwakwala and that audience participation is encouraged make these meetings much more comfortable. The

Anglican service, by contrast, is formal, mechanical, subdued and ritualistic, with a minimum of participation by members of the congregation.

The indigenous religious practices and beliefs of the Kwakiutl revolved around the acquisition of and right to supernatural or spirit power. Winter ceremonials were the occasion at which individuals publicly demonstrated their prerogatives in the religious dance "societies," especially in the *ts^eiqa*, "red cedar bark dance." The Kwakiutl had no belief in a single supreme being, but rather in many spirit forms, some of which inhabited the body of different animals, and others of which were purely spiritual. They also believed that humans have a spirit which leaves the body at death and goes to the spirit world. Spirits were believed to live in villages similar to those on earth.

The first Western religious influence came through Catholic traders, explorers and missionaries. Later the Anglicans became the dominant religious force in the Gilford region, and more recently Pentecostals and others have had a strong impact. The first missionary activities at Gilford were Anglican, and a mission school was in operation there from about 1889 to 1912. Reverend Herbert Pearson, one of the first missionaries at Gilford, gave us the following account about religious education among the villagers during the years he served both Gilford and Kingcome:

> Most evenings I went into different houses and read from the four Gospels, sang Hymns which had also been translated by Mr. Hall, and said Prayers from the English Church Prayer Book. Sometimes quite a number would gather around the fire and sing. Another difficulty was the Winter dances and Potlatch, held during the winter. For three weeks in January they would have their red bark dances, so called because every single individual would wear a strip of red bark around the forehead. These would last three weeks almost day and night. I have known them to continue for 36 hours on end. During that time the children would not attend school.
>
> On Sunday mornings I held service using of course the translated Prayer Book, there would be a fair number present, adults and children. Sometimes the whole tribe would leave for another village (Alert Bay or Fort Rupert, Village Island) or other for Potlatch and stay weeks. Thus it was almost impossible to have any real continuance in anything.

Authority, Power-Prestige, and Friendship

Formal authority within the village at Gilford is vested in the Band council, which is equivalent to a local government body in a rural municipality.[5] Even though the Gilford Island Band came under the provisions of the elective-system in 1957, as specified by the *Indian Act*, a Band council was not established at Gilford until 1961. Councils are concerned with all matters that affect the well-being of Band members, and they are accorded authoritative rights and obligations over the Band by the Department of Citizenship and Immigration. The intent of the Canadian government in instituting this system was to encourage the Indians

---

[5] The term Band refers to a group of Indians who share a common interest in specified tracts of land called Reserves and/or given monetary assets known as Band funds.

to become more involved in their own well-being. But many decisions such as who may join the Band, leasing Reserve land to lumber companies, the expenditure of Band funds, and the introduction of new Band council by-laws are subject to final approval by the Minister of Citizenship and Immigration.

The council system at Gilford is ineffective. One of the principal reasons for this is that the council is an intrusive institution with rules, obligations, responsibilities, rights and expectations that have no counterpart in the customary life of the Kwakiutl. This, in part, contributes to the apathy many villagers feel toward the Band council at Gilford. Moreover, as we describe more fully below, authority vested in the council is inconsistent with village normative standards, including the norm of non-interference. When a villager assumes office he is likely, if he acts in accordance with the norms associated with that status, to violate certain behavior-standards in a community marked by a preexisting network of mutual grievances. Thus, the councillor is apt to lose friends and, to a lesser extent, interpersonal power and prestige. This point, in fact, appears to be one of the most forceful reasons for the ineffectiveness of the Band council at Gilford. That is, in every enduring, face-to-face group, power, prestige and friendship structures emerge. An individual's location within these rank structures is dependent in part on his acceptable performance of social roles—including, of course, his reasonable adherence to normative standards. In general, a person who violates these standards loses power, prestige and friendship. This is what happens to the councillors who act on the authority vested in their position; the council itself thereby becomes less effectual because the members of the community collect additional grievances against those who hold office.

The implications of these facts become clearer after we elucidate the concepts of power, prestige and authority. We define power as the ability to influence the opinions or behavior of others; the more an individual is able to do this, the more power he has. Social power emerges only through the interaction of two or more individuals. To the extent that an individual acquires power within a group, he acquires certain rights over group action which are important in determining the outcome of group activity. Authority includes one type of power; it is the institutionalized right over group or individual action and includes the legitimate right to apply coercive sanctions in threat or fact. Authority is associated with a status or an institutionally defined social position that is identified independently of its occupant. Whereas an individual acquires authority solely by occupying a particular position or status in the social system, power is acquired only through an individual's ability to reward others in specified ways. It is not necessarily associated with any formal status. In every group individuals control differential access to rare and valuable resources which they may distribute among the members of the group, thereby rewarding them. The value of the resources is defined by the normative system of the group.

Prestige is defined here as social rewards—signs of social approval, esteem, respect, admiration or being highly regarded by one's associates. Power and prestige tend to be linked with each other. Thus individuals of high power tend to be individuals of high prestige, and vice versa. Power and prestige also tend to be distributed unevenly throughout the group; that is, no two individuals share the same amount of either. Consequently members of groups may be ranked in both a power structure and a prestige structure, and the two structures tend to be equilibrated or congruent, leading to the concept of power-prestige as distinguished from power *and* prestige.

I designed a sociometric questionnaire to measure power, prestige and friendship within the village just prior to the council election in 1963. I predicted that councillor choices would be made on the basis of both power-prestige and friendship. Since the balloting was to be secret, I asked each person who he thought the three people were who were most capable of acting as councillor, and I asked each person for whom he thought most people in the village would vote. The questionnaire predicted perfectly the new chief councillor and it accurately identified a small pool of villagers from which the other two councillors would be selected. Power-prestige and friendship choices were strongly correlated with councillor choices.[6] We conclude, therefore, that power-prestige and friendship are two crucial bases on which a member of the community is elected to office. In addition, as I expected, one person in the village received far more power-prestige choices than anyone else. He received over 19 percent more power-prestige choices than his nearest competitors—two people tied for second rank—who in turn received almost 2 percent more choices than the person in the third rank. Almost 60 percent of the villagers received only one or no power-prestige choices; they fell in the bottom two ranks of a structure ranging from positions one to thirty-four.

After the election it was clear that both the present and former councillors were high in the power-prestige structure—except for Victor Philip, the former chief councillor, who was in position number eleven in the ranking. Apparently the former councillors were able to maintain their position in the power-prestige structure. The new councillors, Willis Drake (chief councillor), Herbert Philip and Simon Cedar, were in positions one, five and eight respectively. The most noteworthy consequence of having been in a position of authority, however, is found in each man's position within the best-friend rank structure (which ranges from positions one to thirty-nine). Whereas the new councillors, Willis, Herbert and Simon, were in positions one, three and four respectively, the former councillors, Victor and Joseph Abel, were at the bottom of the friendship structure. Edna Moon, the third councillor, was in position number twenty-six. She was able to preserve part of her popularity because, as a woman, she acted least often on the rights and obligations of her status. The great incongruity between the power-prestige and friendship structures of the former councillors has massive implications for the ineffectiveness of the council system at Gilford. And, as we argue below, the former councillors seem to have lost a great deal of their friendship by being councillors.

We must point out, however, that the first chief councillor, Victor, almost certainly did not rank at the top of the best friend structure at the time he was

---

[6] High power-prestige choices are associated with high councillor choices and lower power-prestige choices are associated with low councillor choices. Best friend choices are also associated with the choices given for councillor. Individuals who receive many best friend choices do not necessarily receive many Band councillor choices, but individuals who receive few best friend choices rarely receive any councillor choices.

elected. Possibly he did not rank at the top of the power-prestige structure either because, as we noted earlier, he is a member of the future oriented class and operates on a somewhat different value-standard. Friendship and power-prestige are normally not achieved in situations where an individual violates or is marginal to the norms of the group. The other two councillors are members of the subsisting oriented class and should have ranked at approximately the same level in the two structures. Victor appears to have been elected to office for different reasons than the other two councillors. He was probably selected on the basis of his ability to read, write and speak English fluently, and to a lesser extent because of his acquired power-prestige and friendship within the village. These factors were also taken into consideration by members of the village at the second election. Some villagers expressed concern about Willis' deficiencies in these respects, especially his lack of fluency in English, but he was nevertheless overwhelmingly elected to office.

Authority as manifested in the council system was realigned with the power-prestige and best-friend structures of the village as a result of the election in 1963. Formerly only the power-prestige structure was aligned with the authority system. Presumably friendship was lost, as we said, in the enactment of the rights and obligations contained within the council. In order to operate as councillors, individuals occasionally violated those standards which had led to their original acquisition of friendship. This occurs because the rights and obligations of the council system are inconsistent with many village norms. Again, as we said, an individual in a position of authority has the opportunity to reward or deny rewards to others. He controls access to rare and valuable resources which may be distributed among the members of the group, thereby perpetuating power-prestige; but he may also distribute these in such a way that friendship expectations are violated. Demands are made on councillors which place friendship in jeopardy regardless of the decision made. Members of the village, for example, ask councillors to recommend them for relief. If the request is refused because of insufficient need or because the councillor is angry at the applicant for personal reasons, the latter becomes angry with the councillor. If the request is granted other members of the community become annoyed because they too were not recommended. They expect the councillor to recommend them for relief because they feel that their need is as great as or greater than the first applicant's or because they have as many or more rights based on friendship or kin ties.

Because of these facts we developed the hypothesis that the less an individual of high power-prestige controls and acts on authority, the better he is liked. For example, as we observed earlier, Edna ranked higher in the best-friend structure than the other two councillors. And, as noted, she acted least often on the formal authority granted her by the fact of her office. Because she infrequently acted on the power of authority she was able to maintain friendship ties more easily than the other two councillors. Stanley Philip, tribal chief of the Koeksotenok, provides a second illustration bearing on this hypothesis. He, along with the former councillors, ranked fairly high in the power-prestige structure in 1963, but all four were lowest in the best-friend structure. Stanley controls a great deal of authority in the village and he often acts as the official representative to the Canadian government for Kwakiutl Bands throughout the area. But he is a member of the future oriented class and operates on a different value-standard base from the members of the subsisting oriented group. Thus by violating village norms, he has lost friendship within the community.

The three new councillors had no authority at the time the questionnaire was administered. They all stood high in the power-prestige structure and because they had not yet been elected, they stood highest in the best-friend structure along with three other villagers who had never held office. Ambrose Cedar is the only exception in the village to the rule that the less an individual of high power-prestige controls and acts on authority the better he is liked. Ambrose is one of the highest power-prestige individuals in the village (ranking eighth along with Chief Philip and Simon), but he is at the bottom of the best-friend structure—even though he has never been in a position of authority. We have no explanation for this exception.

Before leaving Gilford in 1963, I made the prediction that the present councillors would lose best-friend choices during their tenure of office, and that by the next election in 1965 they would have fallen toward the bottom of the best-friend structure while maintaining their basic positions in the power-prestige ranking. Field research during the summer of 1964, however, suggested that this prediction needed modification to account for the impact of the chief councillor's wife, Lucy. Most people in the village recognize her as the driving force behind Willis, the chief councillor. In 1963 Lucy ranked among the highest power-prestige individuals in the village; she was also among the highest receivers of best-friend choices. On certain occasions Willis has antagonized members of the community by acting on his authority. Many people blame Lucy for "making him do it." In this way Willis maintained both power-prestige and friendship, but Lucy probably lost friendship. Willis was reelected in the May, 1965, Band council election, thus indicating that he had indeed been able to sustain his position in the power-prestige structure. He also appears to have been able to maintain most of his ties of friendship. Unfortunately we have no information regarding Lucy. As we predicted, however, the other two councillors were replaced by new ones.

An example of the ineffectual nature of the council is found in their inability to sustain a policing system in the village for the enforcement of a 9:00 P.M. curfew on school children and younger children. Different men in the village, including councillors, were assigned the task of sending children home who were found outside after 9:00 P.M., but all of them resigned after a short period, each complaining that he could not control the children of other people. Joe Abel resigned because he could not control the children of Willis Drake, who later accepted the position, then in turn resigned a short time later because he could not control Joe's children. Some men such as Harold Dick, however, are fairly efficient as "policemen" because the children are afraid of them, but parents become antagonistic toward individuals who interfere with their children. Here too the norm of noninterference is in effect.

Councillors are often placed in a situation of structural conflict. By conforming to the rights and obligations of the council system, they violate some of the normative expectations of the villagers. By conforming to the normative expectations of the villagers, they have difficulty performing their duties as councillors. A related set of factors contributing to the ineffectiveness of the council is the fact that the performance expectations of councillors are not crystallized; consequently performance evaluations are inconsistent. Neither the villagers nor the councillors themselves have a clear image of the range of behavior that is appropriate and legitimate for councillors. Certainly there is no consensual validation regarding such behavior. Councillors are inadequately trained or instructed by the Indian Affairs Branch regarding the range of rights and obligations connected with the council system. Councillors are given a manual which assists them but they are not given any practical training. A great deal of mutual misunderstanding exists between councillors and the Indian Affairs Branch, especially the office of the Agency Superintendent.

The effective authority of the councillors is further attenuated and bounded by the normative system in the village which has historical precedence and a great influence on those individuals who are motivated to remain within the network of social relations which characterizes the members of the subsisting oriented class. Villagers recognize the authority of councillors in general, but the normative behavior-expectations are unclear. No standards have developed which coordinate or clearly define the relationship between the authority of the council system and the preexisting normative system.

The effectiveness of the council system is further attenuated because many people in the village criticize the Band council, and councillors are often critical of each other and the village. The former chief councillor, Victor, made the indicative comment that when something goes wrong the council is blamed. "People never put the blame on themselves." The same man was disgruntled because village members did not support him or the other councillors. He insisted that apathy regarding the council and village activities is widespread among the villagers, and cited a number of examples to reinforce his contention; for example, refusal to clean and "modernize" the village, make home repairs, and discipline children. Victor feels that the use of intoxicants is one of the major reasons why none of these tasks was carried out. "They spend their money on beer instead of house repairs and for a boat," and "They think they're doing it behind my back, but I know what's going on." He continued, "People don't even try to cooperate. I've been kidding myself for a long time." From a social interaction point of view, Victor was at a double disadvantage because, first, as a member of the future oriented class he operates on a somewhat different value standard from the other villagers. Second, as a councillor he is in a position of formal authority and the authority of the council system is incongruent with the normative standards of the village. Consequently the fact that he is criticized by other villagers is not surprising. Joe, one of the other councillors, criticized him for not doing his job and stated, "He just doesn't have it up here." Yet when Joe learned that Victor was planning to leave the village he complained, "If you have a good man, who'll do that?" Edna, the third councillor, is volubly antagonistic toward Joe because she feels he carries his authority too far, and she criticizes him for fighting when he drinks. Joe recognizes that the people in the village have grievances against him and admits, "People say I've got a big mouth. That's what they call me." Villagers criticize Joe for looking after the interests of his own family and of himself, but not those of other villagers. Most people recognize his good qualities but talk most often about his bad ones.

Gertie Philip commented that the only time people in the village cooperate with each other is during a school activity. Presumably this is because such activities are generally organized by the teacher. She continued, "The thing about this village is that it's every man for himself." Another person said that villagers expect councillors to do things for them rather than for themselves, and Joe made a similar observation from his point of view. "They're waiting until they're told to do something."

The ineffectiveness of the Band council system at Gilford is duplicated in the apathy toward and ineffectiveness of other task oriented groups. Even though over half the adult males in the village express a moderate to strong interest in village activities, only one-third of them have actually held or presently hold office in any task oriented group. Such groups include the Water (Dam) Committee which is responsible for cleaning and repairing the dam and pipe lines leading into the village. The Dam Committeemen should drain and scrub the dam every six months or more, but in fact it may be cleaned once a year. Water in the dam collects a great deal of debris, including a dead cat several years ago. The Dam Committee is more active than many of the others, however, perhaps because of the importance of fresh water to the village. A Health Committee was established before the Band council was organized. This committee has responsibility for health and sanitation problems within the village. Committeemen are supposed to assure that beaches in front of the village are kept clean and that garbage and other waste material is thrown into the water from the wharf below the low tide mark. The beach in front of the village, however, is strewn with trash of all types. Important changes were made when the committee was first formed in 1960, but little has been done since then. Before that time outhouses and smoke-houses were stationed along the edge of the beach. Since then outhouses have been moved behind the houses against the sharp rise of the mountain. One villager observed that the Health Committee is completely inactive because members "are afraid to try to make people do things." The Sports Club and Breakers Committee are fairly active during the soccer season because of the high level interest and involvement in sports among most of the men. An Anglican Women's Auxilliary (W.A.) was formed several years ago but it became almost defunct after a period of time because the president resigned at the birth of her child and the second president mismanaged the records, including the embezzlement of funds. The W.A. was reorganized by the new minister on the *Columbia* after we left the village in 1963. A Movie Committee was established while we were at Gilford for the purpose of selecting and showing commercial films. Members of the committee operated effectively during that time, and have continued since then.

4

Growing Up Kwakiutl

GERTIE AND MY WIFE were drinking coffee in Gertie's kitchen when they heard a fight outside. Gertie opened the door and yelled at two preschool youngsters tussling over a tricycle. She told the neighbor girl to leave the trike alone and to go home if she did not want to get hit by her son; the trike did not belong to the girl anyway. Gertie grumbled to Evelyn about the behavior of village children. A little while later there were more sounds of children fighting. Gertie got up and yelled at the two children. This time they were both her own and the older boy was beating on his younger brother while the latter feebly tried to take the tricycle. Gertie told the younger boy to leave the trike alone, it was not his and if he did not want to get beaten up by his older brother he should leave things alone that did not belong to him.

The children involved in the dispute over the tricycle that afternoon were two brothers age three and four, and a four-year-old neighbor girl. No attempt was made to control their aggression; in fact Gertie rewarded the actions of the aggressor-owner. As far as Gertie is concerned, the owner of the tricycle has the right to play with it and he is not expected to share his toys. If a child spoils his sibling's possession, villagers consider it to be the owner's fault for leaving the toy unprotected. The owner is expected to protect his property; if he neglects his possessions and they are spoiled, it is his fault.

A second incident which reveals villagers' feelings about rights of ownership occurred in the school during the early part of the year. Since the school has two classrooms but only one teacher, the second classroom is used for storage of extra desks and supplies. Evelyn told the school children that they were not to go there without permission, and we left the door to the storeroom-classroom closed but unlocked. After a few weeks Evelyn went into the storeroom to get some art supplies and noticed most of the pencils, erasers and crayons were gone. She was furious and expressed her anger to the students. I padlocked the second classroom. Evelyn was distressed by the incident because by locking the spare room she had taught the pupils that with locks on doors they could not enter; she wanted them to learn that they should not enter because they were told not to. Later she discovered that the thief had been twelve-year-old Leslie Drake, who, after obtaining the majority of very limited and valued supplies had simply thrown them on the beach. While the villagers clucked sympathetically at the loss, there was an undercurrent of feeling that we were foolish for not attempting to protect school property with a lock rather than with words.

Because the older children were sent to residential school in mid-October, the age range of children at Gilford during our year (except for holidays) extended from infancy to preadolescence and to the age group above sixteen. Major pranks and property destruction were at a minimum; there was no gas sniffing, rarely was beer stolen from drinking parties by youngsters—yet gas sniffing, beer stealing and property destruction were rampant at other villages (cf. Wolcott 1967). We explain this difference as being due to the absence of young adolescents, who are usually the "troublemakers" elsewhere.

Although one frequently hears complaints about destructive children, perhaps accompanied by the recounting of a specific incident, rarely is anything done about it because of the prevailing attitude of noninterference. Ambrose Cedar, for example, observed a gang of kids playing in the big-house and yelled at them to cut it out. The youngsters did not listen and he made no further attempt to stop them. On another occasion two children were breaking Coke and beer bottles against a water faucet. Harold Dick yelled at them to stop, but they did not pay any attention. He turned to me and said, "Those kids don't have ears, I guess." Later the same three-year-olds were doing something else and Norman Philip yelled at them once or twice to quit. He commented to me that, "It's no use yelling at them or getting after them. They don't listen. Beside, if their parents hear me yelling at their kids, they'll just come out and give me a good bawling out. They'll think I've been picking on their kids. Let the kids hurt themselves, I don't care. It's no use!"

That same day Herbert Philip, Harold and I watched several children playing on the porch of an abandoned house. They knocked out one of the windows and after a short time climbed through the window and began playing inside. I made the suggestion that, as councillor, Herb might want to correct the children; he responded that it was none of his business. "It's up to their parents to take care of the kids." All of the known tree burials and grave huts in the nearby cemetery have been demolished by the children. Adults and parents click their tongues, shake their heads and say that children should not do that. "I don't know what's the matter with those kids. They're just haywire, I guess."

Noninterference has its limits, however. Preschool children who wander onto the float are usually told to go home by anyone there and if they do not respond they may be carried off the float. A village rule states that no children are to be on the wharf, but little attention is given to this except in the case of the very young. Occasionally an older child is told to leave, but the issue is seldom pressed.

Women want children; consequently even children who are born as a result of casual sexual affairs are generally accepted. Four youths within the village who resulted from such unions are accepted by other villagers as well as their parents, although comments are occasionally made about their origin if someone becomes angry.

Infants are loved, petted, fondled and held by everyone who is old enough to do so. Teenagers stroll around the village holding or wheeling someone's infant, and children of any age go to the home of an infant and ask if they might take him out. Ten-year-old May Otter proudly recounted to Evelyn each new accomplishment of her infant brother. May and her eight-year-old sister, Betty, spent a great deal of time with their baby brother, and during their parents' drinking parties the two girls took care of him. One day Betty told Evelyn that she wished she could sleep in the classroom. Evelyn asked her why and Betty said she had stayed up late the night before to take care of her brother. Older siblings, both male and female, quite often take care of infants, especially when their parents drink.

A few parents partially abandon their children for periods of time, leaving them in the village to be cared for by someone else while they live away. Viola Abel, for example, locked the doors of her house and left the village without telling anyone. Louisa Cedar, the children's grandmother, cared for them during the two weeks of their mother's absence. Rita Bean has had two children placed in foster homes by court action because a health nurse found one of them alone and sick while her mother was away drinking. But this behavior is very unusual.

The most common form of admonishment applied to children is to hear a parent monotonously repeat, "Don't fool around. Don't fool around." Children generally continue until the tone of "don't fool around" changes, at which time they stop, at least briefly. Some mothers, when they become particularly impatient, yell at their children, "You fucking little bastards! You ass holes!" A mother becomes angry, however, when others do the same to her children. Youngsters quickly become familiar with such language: three girls were on the beach. The oldest, nine, became incensed at the seven-year-old and screamed, "You fucking bastard! You God damned son of a bitch. . . ." The latter retaliated in like manner, but less vociferously. The six-year-old who was with them listened but did not respond.

Around mid-year Leonard Drake, a ten-year-old first grade pupil, came into the teacherage after school to visit. He wandered freely about while Evelyn performed housewifely chores. He left after a while and I reached for our last package of cigarettes; they were gone. Leonard had been the only visitor in our quarters that day, so I went to the village and confronted the youngster who said he had given the cigarettes to his cousin. He went and got them. Willis, the boy's father, is usually extremely mild and soft-spoken, but he overheard the whole conversation and as I left he slapped his son across the face. This is the only incident of which we are aware of a father laying hands on his child when completely sober, and it was so extraordinary that the children talked of it in awed whispers the following days at school. It was still a topic of conversation among adults ten months later.

Another common but more subtle form of discipline is the use of ghost stories. We were unaware of the effectiveness of these stories until the days began to shorten in December. We noticed that as the daylight hours grew short our young visitors disappeared. Once a visiting group of school girls noticed it was getting dark, commented on it and rushed home. We began to realize they were reluctant to be out after dark. Incidents are recounted of ghosts visiting empty houses or peering through windows, sometimes doing minor damage. Many adults, too, are afraid of ghosts, or at least they are willing to impute unexplained events to the mythical person *bukwəs* "wild man of the woods." *Bukwəs* is generally considered to be harmless and has the peculiar ability of moving himself instantly from one location to another a great distance away. The *bukwəs* dance also figures importantly in some of the traditional winter ceremonials.

By age nine or ten, young people begin to identify with sex roles. Girls help around the house; boys are given more freedom to hang around the beach or on the float and occasionally they accompany their fathers fishing. If a man or a group of men go to the store and beer parlor they might take a boy along, but almost never a girl.

Sex role identity is revealed in children's drawings. Girls typically draw pictures of houses and people and sometimes such things as laundry, flowers, and tables with dishes, but they do not draw pictures of traditional Indian designs or boats. Boys at Gilford, on the other hand, most frequently draw pictures of boats and people (men and boys), usually a wharf, sometimes a canoe, fish net or fish and occasionally Indian designs. When the children tell stories about pictures they have created in school each child is able to specify who the people are in the drawings and whose house or boat is represented. None of the stories which accompany the drawings are purely imaginary, and only a few pictures contain fictitious elements, for example, a fence where there is none. The closest children come to making up stories is in the area of humor, where their stories sometimes take the form of *klikwala*, translated very loosely as "just fooling" (or a "white lie"). A child told Evelyn, "Oh, your husband's *really* drunk!" I entered the house at that moment without having had anything to drink. The children were delighted with their joke but were disappointed that I appeared when I did, thus limiting the impact of their *klikwala*. Some Whites misunderstand this form of behavior and decry its usage. The mother of a past teacher in the village, for example, was convinced that the children were inveterate and malicious liars.

Play also reflects sex role identification among children. A favorite activity among boys is to play fisherman. They run along the water's edge with a stick to which a model boat is attached on a line. Occasionally boys drag a piece of net along the ground and pretend to be fishing; on inquiry they will tell whether they are gill netting or purse seining. They sometimes use long reeds or straight sticks to "troll" the soccer field. Other games, except soccer, run in fads and cycles. Sometimes boys play cowboys and Indians using reeds as spears. We were never able to determine the differential attitude toward each, or to determine who usually plays cowboy and who Indian. Judging from the use of spears, however, most of them play Indians. The cowboy role seems to be fairly ignored. Large heavy darts intermittently come into style as do firecrackers and bows and arrows (which Kwakiutl adults do not use). During warm weather boys and girls swim either from the beach or off the float. When they have access to one, older boys enjoy using row boats or canoes and they handle them with proficiency. Children frequently scull the boats with planks or broken oars because they rarely have legitimate access to oarlocks or unbroken oars. Older boys from ten to thirteen often roam around the village, especially when parties are in session.

School represents a discontinuity in the lives of many children since teacher expectations are not reinforced in the home, in the village generally, or by other life experiences. As a result formal education tends to become compartmentalized and disassociated from other life experiences. To the individual it appears to have no basic, immediate relevance for his life at the moment, or for the perceivable future. This has an important bearing on the educational progress of the children and is one set of factors contributing to the high incidence of school drop-outs. School experiences tend to controvert some of the basic learning which takes place in preschool years and in nonschool activities. For example, independence and mild aggression are rewarded in nonschool activities but are negatively sanctioned in the school. The child must learn a form of compliance behavior in the classroom which is not expected out of school; competition with peers rather than aid and cooperation are expected. Concern about delimitable time units leading to the concept of punctuality is important in the educational system and becomes a moral issue for many teachers.

The most important difference between formal education and the cultural system of the villagers lies in the method of learning. This difference creates an important discontinuity in the enculturation process of the children. A Kwakiutl child learns, fundamentally, by observing, performing and then having his behavior rewarded, punished or ignored. Unlike middle-class children, however, the Kwakiutl child initiates most of his own action. He neither expects nor waits for verbal or formal didactic instruction. A child learns to operate a boat and set a net largely through observation of others and subsequently by trying it himself, either in play or by helping his father; he learns to ride a bicycle or to Indian-dance in the same way. For example, Ernest, a young adult, made the indicative comment that no one tells them of their errors when they Indian-dance. Adults or expert dancers do not attempt to make corrections or give instructions. Adults dance and expect the observer to learn the rules from their performance. I noticed the same thing. When I objected about dancing the first time without some indication of the proper way of doing it, Jeffrey Hardy said emphatically, "You'll never learn to dance unless you do it." When I protested further, saying, "Yes, but I need to know what I am *supposed* to be doing," he simply stared at me for a moment and turned away without any further comment. I danced as best I could from watching others. Later when I asked for comments and criticisms regarding my dancing I was told briefly by Frank Bean that I was "too stiff." No elaboration or other correction was offered. Verbal instructions are not totally lacking, however. Once Jeff briefly explained some fine points of dancing to Ernie Amber; Frank observed, "You should have been a teacher. You explained that well."

In the classroom, on the other hand, Kwakiutl children must *learn* to learn through verbal instruction, reading and writing. These methods of learning require language skills in English. Language skills are not as important in the native context; a very small part of becoming a fisherman, for example, is learned through verbal or written instruction.

The fact that the life of the children is structured to a very limited extent within the village constitutes another basic discontinuity between the social and cultural background of the children and the expectations of the school. Whereas parents are permissive toward the behavior of their children, school life is authoritarian and formal. This conflicting situation often imposes as much hardship on the teacher as on the pupils. The lack of structure and the degree of permissiveness by parents may explain, in part, why children bicker, swear, throw things, hit each other and generally pay no attention in the classroom.

Moreover, the children's experience with formal education has been highly inconsistent. Little continuity has existed in the procedures, demands and expectations of past teachers beyond the formal requirements of the Indian Affairs Branch, and the quality of teaching at Gilford has been inconsistent. Children have not had to meet and conform to a uniform set of demands by past teachers which might have allowed them to standardize their behavior and expectations for future ones. To this extent older pupils are not in a position to furnish models for the younger ones regarding appropriate classroom behavior. The inconsistency and discontinuity of educational experiences influence the performance of children. They experience many failures and little pleasure in school activities; as a result some develop a psychological set which predisposes them to anticipate and react to failure in characteristic ways. These include anger, giving up and, in the extreme, not trying in the first place. Many children have a low frustration tolerance for difficult school assignments. They react with anger, or sometimes, they cry if they cannot complete their work with relative ease and they often give up and refuse to try. Evelyn found beginning students were better able to grasp new concepts, commensurate with their age level, than older students. Part of the reason for this lies in the fact that the former have not experienced as many failures and have not developed a negative set toward trying.

One day Leslie Drake pushed Evelyn's patience too far by whistling while she was trying to teach a geography lesson. She told him to stop; he continued to whistle, and the other students became nervously silent. Evelyn walked to Leslie's desk and again told him to stop whistling. He looked her directly in the eye, puckered up and whistled. She slapped him across the face in total frustration and rushed out of the noiseless classroom into the teacherage. After a few moments she wiped her tears and returned to the still quiet classroom. From then on whenever a child went too far the closest part of his anatomy received the back of her hand. Here was a form of punishment expected from teachers and understood both by parents and students. Yet at the end of the year a six-year-old boy who had been spanked fairly often said, "Gee Mrs. Rohner, you nicest teacher we ever had; you never hit us once!"

School routine is further disrupted during periods of heavy drinking. If the children attend school at all they are often too tired to work and sometimes too tense. An increase of the noise level in class is often a good indicator of extensive drinking in the village, and periods of drinking in conjunction with conflict among members of the village are major contributors to the disruption of class-room routine. Willie Moon, who managed to come to school one morning, told Evelyn that he had three hours of sleep the night before. He had five the night before that. His brother Ralph did not come at all. The boys' father, Paul, apparently becomes abusive toward Ralph when the former drinks and, for the past couple of days Ralph had been trying to find a place to sleep where he would be out of Paul's reach.

Classroom control is further complicated by the fact that children reflect and react to tensions within the village. Evelyn often knew from the way the children behaved that a fight or other dispute had erupted in the village. Children carry parental gossip and feelings of animosity into the classroom and they tease or fight with the children of the people toward whom their parents are antagonistic. After Christmas vacation the pupils shunned May and Betty Otter, the children of the man who had broken into the school during our absence. Only by Evelyn's persistent attention to the problem and by forcing the students to talk about it were the two girls reaccepted into the group. For a few days comments had been overt and disruptive as, "Gee I don't want to sit next to you; your father's no good!" At another time the Hardys, grandparents of three school children ages six, nine and ten, excluded Willis Drake from a drinking party. Willis' oldest daughter in school is sharp-tongued and a school leader. She made sure that Jeffrey Hardy's three grandchildren were alternately tormented, picked on and ignored for a few days.

Only under extreme provocation, however, is Leonard Drake, the ten-year-old first grader mentioned earlier, ever picked on by the other students—although he would be fair game because he cries easily. Actually the whole village feels protective of Leonard, and their greatest wrath at a previous teacher was because he had dragged Leonard home from school by the ear. Evelyn too had to be careful in her handling of Leonard if she wanted to avoid student hostility.

Frequently we heard from city dwellers that, whereas the Indians may not know about "Dick and Jane," they certainly know all about their village environment. This is untrue. The younger pupils express amazement that animals once lived in the shells found on the beach. They were surprised to discover they could make pots from the clay deposit we found near a stream at one end of the village. And none of them had ever looked closely at a snake. One day, for example, I came into the classroom with a small garter snake; the children screamed in fright. Eventually they calmed down and the snake was placed among the slugs and moss in a terrarium. The pupils spent the rest of the day lying on the floor, noses pressed to the glass, while Evelyn read to them anything she could find on snakes. Even at the level of the most elementary readers children are exposed to things which they have never seen or about which they have never heard. A few of the children have never seen an automobile, and most of them have never seen a horse or the other farm animals which are included in the vocabulary of early readers. At a more sophisticated level most of the children have never heard of an elevator, and the idea of an escalator—steps which can continuously ascend or descend—is strange indeed!

Prior to our arrival in the village many of the younger children had never been to a movie. One mother reported that when she first took her two sons to a movie in Alert Bay they continually asked, "What's that? What's that?" A second child, Adam Bean, was enthralled with colored slides which I had taken of the village, the surrounding area, and Vancouver. Evelyn reported that he was so excited, "He almost climbed into the screen." Adam, an eight-year-old boy, had never seen Alert Bay, but he was the only child of his age who had not.

Commercial movies were shown in the village during our year of research. Those who had the money or could borrow it often went to both showings. Two movies drew particularly favorable attention from the villagers, both adults and children. One of them involved a White man who became a Teton-Sioux after surviving the run of the arrow, and the second movie related to a White adolescent who had been captured as a child by a group of Indians on the Delaware. All commercial movies were selected from an annotated list by several men in the village. Even though we could not determine the educational impact of movies among the children, it should not be underestimated because the boundaries of their social universe were extended. The boundaries were further expanded through occasional slide shows given by such people as the doctor on the *Columbia*, the ship belonging to the Columbia Coast Mission. The children were impressed, for example, with a piece of human hair when they saw it under the doctor's microscope.

Many adults and adolescents remember school with distaste because of repetitive failures in conjunction with other negative experiences. Children typically approach school with substantial ambivalence and many Indian students leave school at the minimum age of sixteen because of these feelings. An adolescent girl who had dropped out of school could remember only one incident which she described as fun in all her years at school. She probably is not atypical. According to the Indians these observations are as true of experience in residential schools as in the village day schools.

A child learns about the major roles in the social system at a fairly young age. He knows what his parents do and how they do it; he knows about kinsmen and non-kin residents of the village; he has attended and sometimes participated at least marginally in all the recurrent activities of the village; he is aware at least vaguely of all the important relationships and events encountered by those around him; he believes that when he grows older he too will be a fisherman. A girl believes she will be a wife and mother. The child is prepared to activate these roles at the appropriate time. In short, adulthood holds no mystery for Kwakiutl children. To this extent formal education received in the classroom does little to realistically or importantly prepare most of the children, from their point of view, for the future.

Changes in status are not clearly marked among the Kwakiutl; although starting school, quitting school and marriage are incidents which mark changes in role behavior. When a male reaches sixteen and is no longer required to attend school he generally drops out. Girls attend school beyond sixteen if facilities are open to them.

Adolescent girls, unless married, are accorded adult status at a later age than males. They usually live with a family, frequently but not always their parents, and their activities are closely watched since the role of adult woman revolves around the home and child rearing. If a girl is unmarried there are insufficient indicators of her adult status. Males, on the other hand, are mobile and independent at an earlier age and are in a position to act out adult roles independent of marriage ties, hence they are accorded adult status at an earlier age. According to one of our informants, girls are thought of as "ladies" after their first menstruation, but being a woman in this sense does not imply full status as an adult female. Gertie described to Evelyn her feelings about the first time she menstruated. She was at a residential school and said that one of the staff members there made the girls feel dirty and bad about it. Few girls know about menstruation before it happens, apparently, and mothers and daughters or unmarried peers do not talk about such subjects very often. Another of our informants said that women know very little about personal matters before they are married.

Free time and its management create minor problems for adolescents as well as for some young married people. Problems typically take the form of restlessness and occur most notably during the slack economic season, the period between clam digging and summer fishing. Teen-age girls agree that winter is the best time in the village because everyone is there and they have more to do. A portion of each day is unoccupied by household chores or other tasks, especially during the evening, but during the slack season the villagers also have quite a lot of free time during the day. This free time is filled in various ways. Women spend a large part of it within their homes often doing nothing more than listening to the radio and gazing out a window. Several teen-age girls frequently stroll around the paths of the village together. Young men occasionally do the same, but men and women do not mix publicly unless they are married or courting. During the 1962–1963 school year some of the adolescent girls who had dropped out of school visited my wife several evenings each week, strolled around, helped their parents and relatives with household chores and talked of and sometimes did visit relatives in other villages. In the spring these girls organized their own soccer team.

During our year at Gilford there were a number of unmarried males in their late teens and early twenties. These men fished as crew members on commercial seine boats in the summer; during the fall they were generally idle, strolling around the village, attending dances at the school and visiting the missionary to play checkers. In the winter they dug clams, drank, danced, and frequently spent their time "walking around." In the spring, however, they trained for soccer. Each soccer team is a recognized group with its own uniforms, name and equipment, and competition among teams is strong. The members of the Gilford team— the Breakers—often practice from one to two hours a day. Other teams come to Gilford on weekends for a practice game or the Breakers may go elsewhere. Kingcome and Gilford play in serious competition each year during the month of May at Kingcome. A second major soccer event is the May Sports competition in Alert Bay. The largest and most serious sports event of the year, however, is the Native Celebration or June Sports in Alert Bay. June Sports typically lasts three days and involves many activities such as a parade, special Indian programs, athletic events of which soccer is the highlight, and various contests. June Sports is important because, as we said earlier, it also marks the beginning of the new salmon fishing season. Other free time activities, except drinking, are of significantly less importance in terms of their impact on village life. Young men sometimes play cards in the evening if several interested people can be found, and many people take naps during the day.

The transition from adolescence to adulthood is often dramatized by marriage. Courtship is an important activity during adolescence. Unmarried couples stroll around the village after dark, pausing now and then in the shadows. Dances in the school furnish another occasion when men and women may be together, but little overt romantic behavior is manifested in such a public setting. Romances are often short lived, but when they become serious the individuals involved may begin sleeping together fairly regularly. As we noted above, however, a girl who sleeps with too many men soon acquires a bad reputation and she becomes the butt of a considerable amount of criticism and gossip. The teen-age daughters of Edna Moon, for example, were accused of leading Jennie Drake's daughter astray. Edna was disturbed and angry about the accusations. An elderly informant told me that at one time it was shameful for a girl not to be a virgin at the time of marriage. He confesses that he does not know what the dominant attitude is now.

Albert Philip, a nineteen-year-old youth, lived with a twenty-one-year-old woman, Darlene Moon, in Darlene's parents' home during part of the winter and spring of 1963. They later decided to get married and, as expressed to us in a letter from Gertie Philip, "[They are] I think getting married as Darlene says its Albert's baby she is carring. they are both scared to tell Albert's parents. yet [the parents] know already about it." Albert's father later wrote, "I have conceded to have him married, so we would have a chance to have both, with us to try to adjust them to a more stable way of living." After the wedding Gertie wrote, "the wedding really was nice. Albert and Darlene are living with [Albert's parents], I think they aren't sorry about Albert finely marring Darlene as I sort of talked them into consenting because Albert was just living with Darlene."

The attitude of acceptance toward common-law alliances is further illustrated by Fred Drake, a twenty-two-year-old man who began living with a girl, Ruby, who was separated from her husband. The couple lived with Ruby's parents. Fred became a marginal member of both the young men's group and the adult males'. After they had lived together for a year, one of Ruby's younger brothers commented, "They should get their own house. They're married now." And as their year of common-law alliance progressed, Fred was identified more and more with the adult married men.

PART TWO

Potlatch Period

5

Traditional Social Organization

D URING THE POTLATCH PERIOD from about 1849 until almost 1930 the Kwakiutl were, in principle, totally rank stratified: each tribe was ranked in relation to each other tribe; each major tribal subdivision, the numima, was ordered in relation to each other numima, and each individual within each numima was ranked in relation to every other individual.[1] In addition, persons in different numimas were ranked relative to each other. Within this idealized serial ordering, however, there was sometimes equivocation and uncertainty regarding the proper rank-placement of any given unit: a tribe, a numima or, particularly, an individual. This was most notably true of the correct ranking of different persons vis-à-vis each other in different numimas. There was nonetheless a strain toward this ideal rank-structure model.

Table 3 reveals something about the nature of these facts. The Kwakiutl proper, the *KwaigyuL*, were the highest ranking tribe among all the southern Kwakiutl tribes. The Mamalelekala were ranked second and the Four Tribes of Gilford—the Tsawatenok, Koeksotenok, Guauaenok and Hahuamis—were in positions seven through ten respectively. The Mamalelekala were comprised of five serially ordered numimas, and in the late nineteenth century each numima had from six to forty-two ranked, hereditary, positions signaled by a discrete name for each position. The men holding these names formed the "nobility" among the Mamalelekala. This ranking was done largely for potlatch purposes where no two people could have their names called simultaneously to receive gifts, or where no two persons could sit in the same rank ordered seat at a potlatch, feast, or winter ceremonial.

Not only were the Kwakiutl rank stratified, but they were also segregated into semi-equilibrated social strata. Whether these strata should be called classes

---

[1] Elsewhere (1967:27) I wrote that the correct term designating the tribal subdivisions of the Kwakiutl is numimot (*nEᵋmī'mot*). The term actually refers to the members of the tribal subdivision, not to the subdivision itself. The term numima (*nEᵋmī'ma*) correctly identifies the subdivisions, although in practice some Kwakiutl do not distinguish between these terms anymore.

TABLE 3.
PARTIAL RANK ORDER OF KWAKIUTL TRIBES, NUMIMAS AND HEREDITARY NAMES
(SOCIAL POSITIONS): 1895[a]

Partial Rank Ordering of Tribes	Ranked Numimas (Mamalelekala)	Partial Ordering of Ranked Names in Numimas
1. Kwakiutl (*KwaigyuL*)		
2. Mamalelekala	1. *Kuek*[u] (Eagle)	1. 2. Creating Trouble All Around . . . 4. The Great One Always Alone in World . . . 6.
	2. *TEmɬtEmɬEls* (Ground Shakers)	1. Four-Fathom Face . . 5. From Whom Property Comes . . . 15. Whose Body Is All Wealth . . 32.
	3. *WiwomasgEm* (The Noble Ones?)	1. To Whom People Paddle . . 15. Whose Property Is Eaten in Feasts . . 21.
	4. *ᵋWālas* (The Great Ones)	1. . . 4. Always Giving Potlatch . . 7. From Whom Coppers Are Obtained . . 42. Around Whom People Assemble

TABLE 3. (*continued*)

5. Mämalelaqäm (The Real Maleleqala)	1. Catching Salmon
	⋮
	13. Always Giving Blankets Away While Walking
	⋮
	30. Getting Too Great

3. Nimkish

⋮

7. Tsawatenok
8. Koeksotenok
9. Guauaenok
10. Hahuamis

⋮

---

[a] After Boas 1897:339–340, 1996:39; Rohner 1967:73

or status groups is, in part, a matter of definition. For ease of presentation, however, we prefer to call them classes.[2] The Kwakiutl use two terms to designate these social and ceremonial classes. The first is *naqsala,* "nobility," and the second is *xamala,* "commoner."[3] At one time the Kwakiutl also had slaves who were usually war captives from other tribes. Slaves contributed little to the traditional social system except to give prestige to their owners; we give them no further attention.

Rank and class were determined primarily by inheritance—the inheritance of socially validated names and "privileges" such as the right to sing certain songs, use certain carvings or designs, wear certain ceremonial masks and perform certain dances. Associated privileges included the right to sit at a particular place during a potlatch, to have one's name called at a certain point in a sequence, and to receive greater or lesser amounts of property dependent on one's overall position in the rank structure. Those who had no or few (or unimportant) of these attributes were the commoners and those who had many or important ones were the nobility. Both noblemen and to a lesser extent commoners were differentiated into fine gradations of rank. At a certain point the distinction between low ranking noblemen and high ranking commoners sometimes became blurred. Commoners, however, were excluded from important participation in the winter ceremonial dance

[2] The Kwakiutl are neither rank nor class stratified today in any important manner. Most of the data presented here relate to the Gilford Island Kwakiutl and cognate Bands around the turn of the century.

[3] The term nobility is not a good gloss of the Kwakiutl term *naqsala,* but it has been fairly well standardized in the anthropological literature so we continue to use it. Perhaps a better translation would be aristocracy, upper class or simply, chiefly class.

societies. And as expressed to us by one of our informants, "You're *xamala* if you don't have anything behind you for the potlatch."

The Kwakiutl also recognized class distinctions in other ways, for example in their social and kinship terminology. Several years ago two noblemen argued over a log for firewood. One accused the other of acting just like a *xəxis*, that is, as a *xamala* or commoner. The term *xamala* means, literally, an orphan. Neither an orphan nor an illegitimate child could be a nobleman because neither had anyone from whom he could claim the requisite names and privileges. The term *xamala* itself was sometimes used as a term of abuse or derogation by the nobility. Kinship terminology supplies a further illustration. A nobleman's daughter, *qidiL*, was referred to differently from a commoner's daughter, *tsedak*; moreover, a noblewoman who married a nobleman was called *modziL*. Out of respect to her huband, however, a commoner woman was referred to as *modziL* if she married a nobleman. Members of the Kwakiutl nobility married most often among themselves, thus perpetuating many of the important names and privileges in the chiefly class. According to one of our informants, noblemen also interacted socially more often among themselves than with commoners. In fact as a child one of the highest ranking men in Fort Rupert is reported to have been allowed to play only with other high ranking children. His parents would not let him play with commoner children.

Kwakiutl social organization has changed radically in the last half century. Today there is no significant tendency to associate only with members of the same class. In fact the rank and class system has broken down. Older adults in the village remember the social stratum to which they traditionally belonged, but many of the younger do not know where they would be placed. Spontaneous remarks sometimes made by members of the community, however, suggest that past traditions are not totally ignored; for example, Flora Abel, her son Andy, and several others were drinking. Andy became abusive toward his mother and she ran out of the house into a second house where another party was in progress. She asked some of the men to help her, but they ignored her request. She cried at a table, repeating over and over, "He can't do that to me. I'm *naqsala*! He can't do that. . . ."

We do not know of any children at Gilford today who have validated privileges. This further attests to the major changes in the Kwakiutl social system over the past decades. Over 70 percent of the men in the twenty to thirty-nine age group do not have any validated privileges, whereas almost 90 percent of the men who are forty and over do. A comparable trend exists regarding validated names: only 35 percent of the men from twenty to thirty-nine remember having any, and they have only one each, whereas more than 90 percent of the men who are forty or older have from one to four names, or more.

As we said, rank was acquired largely through inheritance, either through the father or the mother. But it could also be acquired through adoption. For example, if a grandfather wanted to make sure that certain of his important rights and privileges remained in his numima, he could adopt one of his grandchildren and transmit the names and privileges to him in a potlatch, or if a family line was threatened with extinction a child could be adopted and bequeathed names and privileges. The Kwakiutl also had other means of acquiring rank or, obversely, of transmitting names and privileges. One of the most unusual of these was through fictitious marriages. Boas (1966:55) describes such a situation:

> Difficulties arise when no daughter is available through whose marriage a name may be transmitted to her offspring. It cannot be done directly through the marriage of a son. For instance, a certain chief had two wives and only one son. The son married two wives but had no issue. Then the chief "turned the left side of his son's body" into a woman and gave him the name belonging to the eldest daughter of his line. Soon another chief, who wished to get the names belonging to the father of the man whose one side had been turned into a woman, wooed her, and the whole marriage ceremony was performed. The young man stayed in his father's house, but when the time for the transfer of names occurred, the appropriate ceremony was performed just as though a real marriage had been performed. Sham marriages of this type are the device resorted to in such cases.
>
> If there is no son, the father may call his foot, or one side of his body his daughter. The marriage ceremony is performed as though these were the women married, and the names are transferred in the usual manner.

At a marriage potlatch the father-in-law gave names and other wealth to his son-in-law to hold in trust for the former's grandchildren. Sons-in-law, however, often used these names for their own purposes—such as acquiring a position in a second numima—before transmitting them to their children. Still another, but unusual, means of acquiring rank and privileges during part of the last century was by murdering the man whose possessions one wanted. The murderer then claimed the names and other prerogatives of the vanquished. The evidence for this method of obtaining rank is uncertain, however, except in the case of acquisition of ceremonial privileges, such as the right to certain songs and dances in the winter ceremonial complex.

As we have seen, most rights and privileges were ordered in a prestige hierarchy. The overall social stature of a person was dependent on the number and importance of the privileges he could legitimately claim and these rights functioned to mark one person off from another. The value of these prerogatives was defined by the frequency and extravagance of the potlatches at which they were used. The most eminent person within the numima—as defined by his rights and privileges—was the chief, and the highest ranking person in the leading numima was sometimes designated tribal chief, at least by Whites. There was little difference between the numima chief and the second ranking man, or between the second and third ranking men, but an enormous social distance separated the highest ranking person from a person with no or only unimportant prerogatives.

The anthropological literature is inconsistent in its description of chiefs. Sometimes the term designates the numima head—the ranking person in the numima power-prestige structure—and sometimes it refers to all members of the nobility. Unless otherwise noted, we use the term in the former sense. Ideally the numima chief was the oldest son in a line of oldest sons traced back to a real or mythical ancestor, but if the oldest child were a girl she would be considered the ranking person, following the rule of primogeniture. The Kwakiutl, however, preferred males in the ranking positions because women were excluded from hereditary office in some of the ceremonial societies, regardless of their rank. The woman who succeeded to the office of chieftainess was given a man's name and even though she became a man socially, she was expected to transmit the names and other prerogatives which qualified her for the position to her son when he was an adult. If the oldest son died without heirs of his own, his younger siblings ranked in order of their birth, or if the oldest brother was not considered to be competent his younger brother might be able to claim his name and position.

Younger children of a chief received fewer and less important privileges than the oldest child. They were, therefore, somewhat lower in rank. Nonetheless they commanded respect, in part because they were potential heirs of the eldest brother even though they did not usually claim any formal status themselves. Over the generations children of younger siblings often slipped in the overall rank structure because at each successive generation they had less symbolic wealth to distribute. From this point of view many commoners were simply less fortunate kinsmen of the nobility. The highest chief's younger brother was usually not chief of the second ranking numima. This position was inherited by the person who claimed descent by primogeniture from his predecessor—sometimes, as in the case of two related Koeksotenok numimas, the man who could most legitimately claim descent through the senior genealogical line back to the second brother of the mythological founder of the tribe. The same principle of primogeniture held true for all other titled, chiefly positions.

The political status of chief implies little more than preeminent social status. But even though chiefs had little coercive authority, their position as numima administrator was a responsible one. Chiefs, along with other important members of the numima who acted as advisors, were responsible for making decisions regarding the timing and utilization of numima fishing grounds, clover beds, berry fields and hunting territory; it was also their responsibility to insure that the correct rituals were performed before this property was exploited. In addition they were the trustees of numima ceremonial prerogatives such as songs, carvings, names and dances. And it was chiefs who had the major responsibility for giving potlatches.

The chief's power and prestige were not his to be enjoyed effortlessly. In fact his stature could fluctuate and it was dependent on the support of others. This support in turn was contingent on three factors: his potlatching record, his generosity, and the importance of his kin group (Barnett 1968:46ff). A chief inherited the right to his position, but he had to assume it publicly and he was expected to maintain if not improve the prestige of that position through lavish potlatching. His numimot—members of his numima—were concerned about his success because his public performances reflected on them; they had a personal interest as well as a substantial financial investment in him. Thus, a chief was dependent on others for at least part of his potlatch resources because, often, he could not personally marshal together the material wealth needed to put on a munificent potlatch. For the most part a chief's numimot willingly contributed, not because they had to but because they wanted to. Moreover, the men in his numima regularly contributed a portion of the fish, seals, or other animals they caught, and women gave tribute to his wife by relinquishing a portion of the berries and roots they collected.

High ranking Kwakiutl were involved in a complex debt and credit obligation system. Single or double woolen Hudson's Bay blankets, valued at fifty cents and one dollar and fifty cents respectively, constituted the currency-standard among the Kwakiutl. The value of other items was measured in terms of them. Interest was charged on all but very short-term loans. After less than six months six blankets had to be returned for every five borrowed; seven blankets had to be repaid for every five borrowed at the end of six months. The Kwakiutl collected 100 percent interest on loans of one year or more; the debtor was obligated to return ten blankets for every five that he borrowed (Boas 1966:78). Moreover, a person who had poor credit might pawn his name for a year during which time the name could not be used. The debtor paid back one hundred blankets for the thirty he received for his name, over 300 percent interest. A man could, however, receive a short-term loan without interest, depending on his credit rating and the feelings of his creditor. Successful Kwakiutl were involved in borrowing as both creditors and debtors. A prospective potlatcher, for example, called his own and other groups together for a feast at which time he loaned blankets to selected, responsible participants. To be chosen to receive such a loan meant the recipient was respected by the donor and recipients were obligated to repay the debt with interest when the host was ready to give his potlatch.

The system of debts and loans worked well because the Kwakiutl did not acquire wealth for its own sake. To hoard was shameful, almost unthinkable. Wealth was important only insofar as it could be publicly displayed and redistributed in feasts and potlatches—thereby raising the esteem of the donor.

Generosity was the second source of a chief's power and prestige. As we said earlier, a chief's numimot supported many of his activities, but he in turn was generous to them. Whenever he called his numinot together to announce or discuss some important issue he feasted them. He frequently did the same before and after potlatches as well, and he fed his supporters when they completed some valuable service for him. As Barnett (1968:49) writes, "a chief flourishes—gains adherents at home and acquires esteem abroad—through his reputation for liberality."

The third source of a chief's power lay in the strength and importance of his kin group which included affinal kinsmen (relatives by marriage). The preeminent social and kinship unit among the Kwakiutl was the numima, an ambilineal corporate descent group, membership being acquired through either or both parents and traced back ambilaterally through successive generations to the mythical or real ancestor of the numima. Noblemen within a numima believed they were descended from the same founding ancestor. According to one of our older informants, however, a man could "ask a stranger to be his numimot, if he wanted to." This normally involved the acquisition of a name and other privileges belonging to the numima. A child was assigned to the highest ranking position available to either of his parents. Generally if both parents were of the same overall rank, the first child was assigned to the numima in which his father had his highest rank, reflecting a preference for the patriline. Subsequent children were given successively lesser positions depending on those available to their parents.

Numimas were corporate groups because each had a name, held rights over fishing locations and other sites of economic importance and maintained certain ceremonial privileges. The members of these groups shared a set of oral traditions regarding its place of origin and adventures of the numima ancestors which usually explained why the numimot had the right to claim specified privileges. In addition each numima shared a set of factual or quasi-factual tales of recently acquired privileges. And each numima claimed ownership of one or more multi-family dwellings in its winter village.

In an important sense the structure of numimas is best described not in terms of people but in terms of a series of ranked positions forming the nobility. According to Boas (1966:50) the thirteen Kwakiutl tribes in the Gilford region shared 658 "seats," "standing places," or ranked positions. The Indian population in British Columbia barely escaped being obliterated from the time of the first European contact until 1890; gradual population attrition continued until about 1929 when the Kwakiutl began to increase slowly in numbers. Whites brought with them measles, smallpox, tuberculosis, influenza and venereal diseases, thus accounting for this gross decimation. Codere (1950:50) estimates that only 637 of the 1597 people surviving in 1898 were sixteen years old or more—not enough to fill the 658 seats in the Kwakiutl social system. As a result men were able to claim more than one standing place within a numima, and they could have positions in more than one numima—even though they tended to maintain primary affiliation with one numima. This created the anomalous situation where a nobleman, as potlatch host in one numima, could call out in rank order the names of his guests in the second numima. In the process he would call one of his own names as a member of the second numima.

Each numima consisted of one or several extended family household groups living within its own localized section of the village. The Kwakiutl lived in massive, beamed, multi-family dwellings, usually lined side-by-side facing the water. The one remaining multi-family dwelling (called big-house or *gyux*) at Gilford is no longer employed as a residence but is now used as a place for Indian dancing and other community activities. It is 70 feet long, 45 feet wide and about 20 feet high. The shake roof is supported by massive, hand-hewn beams about 3 feet in diameter, and the entire roof section is supported by four finely carved posts about 3 feet across. The frame of a smaller big-house stands next to it. The vertical poles supporting the four beams are carved; the figures on two of them represent the mythological origin and later incidents in the history of the Koeksotenok.

Big-houses were inhabited by several related families, a man—the "house chief"—his wife and children along with his younger brothers, their wives and children; other kinsmen and visitors sometimes lived with them. Each nuclear family (a man, his wife and their children) had a fireplace of its own within the big-house and a central fireplace was usually placed in the middle of the earthen-floored building. The smoke dissipated through moveable planks in the roof. Each nuclear family had its own bedroom-cubicle appended along the wall on a platform circumscribing the interior of the house. A house could contain ten or more of these compartments, but more often it contained only four. The entire assemblage was removed to seat participants for feasts and potlatches.

Many numimas in different tribes were unrelated except by later inter-

Frame of a big-house

marriage. A few of them, however, as with two Koeksotenok numimas, counted the separate family lines descended from two mythological brothers as separate numimas. Boas (1966:43), for example, gives one abbreviated version of the tale connecting these numimas: "Head-Winter-Dancer [Tseikami] came from the sky as a thunderbird. His four sons settled in four villages. The youngest one, a warrior, stayed with his father. Two of the others became ancestors of two [numimas] of the [Koeksotenok] . . ." In other cases mythological brothers could be the progenitors of different tribes. The Hahuamis, the second tribe formally constituting the Gilford Island Band, and the Tsawatenok, one of the Four Tribes of Gilford, illustrate this point. This tale was given to me by an elderly Tsawatenok

Interior of the big-house

Kwakiutl sailing canoes (E.C. Curtis)

man; it clearly contains several recent Biblical intrusions such as a reference to
God and to the time before there was light on earth.

Qawadeilakala with his four children and his younger brother *Koleili* lived before
there was light on the earth. They heard the voice of God who said that they were
to go and find a place which they could claim as their own. The voice promised them
the cloak of a wolf for ease of transportation [i.e., transformed them into wolves].
The two brothers and four children came first to Kingcome. The older brother claimed
lalaq, a site up Kingcome River as his own. *Koleili* did not want to share the same
site with his brother, so he moved on to look for his own place. He travelled to
lax·oh "clear-water" and then to Wakeman River. He stayed there for three or
four years and then he returned to the Kingcome River to meet his brother. *Koleili*
asked *Qawadeilakala* what the sound of the bird was like that the latter heard at his
location. *Qawadeilakala* said that it sounded like *dzawadasli* (?), so the younger
brother said that from this time on *Qawadeilakala* would be known as *dzawadEeinox^u*
[Tsawatenok]. *Qawadeilakala* then asked *Koleili* what the sound of the bird was like
that the latter heard in his valley, and *Koleili* answered *ha^ewala* so *Qawadeilakala*
said that from this time on you will be known as [Hahuamis]. The two brothers
then separated again, each to his respective location.
    Later the two brothers met again and each wanted to try out his magical powers
on the other to see which was greater. They had a magic rock called *x·welk* which
they threw back and forth to each other. The two brothers, who wore hemlock
cloaks, stood at quite a distance from each other while they threw and caught the
rock. The older brother missed it on the third throw, and it landed on the right
hand side of the river at *x·wellek*, a little above *tsætsala*. The mountain where the
older brother missed the rock is now called *x·welLeix*. Because the older brother lost
the game, he took one of his children and pulled him apart into many pieces and
turned the pieces into feathers which became birds to fly all over the earth. The
younger brother went back to Wakeman. *Qawadeilakala* returned to his place and
then started moving down the river to the present Kingcome village site. When he
arrived there he saw what looked like worms but were really oulachon fish. He saw

another man there who claimed to have come from the moon. The latter gave him instructions what to call the oulachons, *mənmənLilaga*. *Qawadeilakala* had a dog which caught and ate an oulachon. The dog died. The man from the moon told *Qawadeilakala* to fear not; "The fish will mean a great deal when the time comes. They will do a great wealth." And then the man from the moon left. *Qawadeilakala*, who still had his wolf powers, wondered if he were alone on the earth with his brother, so he howled like a wolf. After the third howl he heard an answer from *xˑoyalas* [Hoyalas, extinct group at Quatsino] so he found that someone else was on earth besides himself and his brother. The Hoyalas howled too and *hausit*, a people on the West Coast, answered him.

Numimas were not always stable. Dissatisfied nuclei of closely related kinsmen sometimes spalled off from larger numimas to form their own. Of course they had to publicly validate the new numima by giving a potlatch. On other occasions internal dissensions were generated when a chief failed in generosity, became overbearing or was faulted on other counts. Here too a numima could disintegrate into two or more numimas. Moreover, ambitious noblemen, secondary chiefs or house chiefs could create a disaffected faction and break away. These new numimas, however, remained within the larger structure of the tribe—although each maintained a large element of its sovereignty, conceding little economic or political autonomy to the tribe.

Originally numimas appear to have been independent village-communities which eventually congregated at a single village site along with other numimas to form a tribe. Tribal structure, then, represents little more than an aggregation of several numimas within a common winter village.[4] Tribes did, however, function as a collectivity for ceremonial purposes—feasts, potlatches and winter ceremonials —and they did act, on rare occasions, as units of defensive action against other tribes, especially non-Kwakiutl. The Bella Coola raid is one of the most famous illustrations of this in the history of the Kwakiutl.

Around the fall of 1857 a ranking Bella Coola (another Northwest Coast tribal group) man, his wife and probably several other families were at Bond Sound near Gilford, perhaps to catch herring but more probably to collect roots and to trade. Several Koeksotenok families were also at the site. One of the Koeksotenok women stole a very valuable hamatsa whistle belonging to the ranking Bella Coola couple, but no retaliation was taken then, even though the theft was a capital offense. The following autumn the Bella Coola attacked Gilford in revenge. Boas (1897:427) gives the following account of the raid:

[The Bella Coola] landed above the village . . . and hauled their canoes ashore. Late in the evening they sent spies out to examine the village. About midnight, when all the [Koeksotenok] were asleep, the [Bella Coola] launched their canoes and divided. One-half went to the east end of the village, and one-half to the west end. They stayed in their canoes not far from the beach until it was almost daylight. It was foggy. As soon as it grew daylight they landed and many men went to the rear of the houses. As soon as they were ready the most courageous warriors broke into the doors of the houses and speared men, women and children. Whoever tried to escape through the rear door was speared by the men stationed there. Others

---

[4] Tribes split up into constituent numimas during the summer and migrated to their fishing sites.

of the [Bella Coola] looked after the valuable property and put it into their canoes. Now the [Koeksotenok] were all killed. Only seven men and five women were left. Then the [Bella Coola] set fire to the houses. Their canoes were deeply loaded with men's heads. They went home. At that time people of different tribes had stayed at [Gilford]; [Mamalelekala, Tlauitsis, Nimkish, and Nakoaktok], all guests of the [Koeksotenok]. They were all slain by the [Bella Coola] and also some who belonged to the [KwaigyuL]."

(Brief archeological excavations that I undertook in the village suggest that the Bella Coola probably also dismembered the bodies of their victims.)

A few days later the Fort Rupert Kwakiutl (*KwaigyuL*) organized a retaliatory war party, including four Mamalelekala war canoes, six Nimkish, two Tlauitsis, and eight Tsawatenok. In addition the subtribes of the *KwaigyuL* contributed sixteen canoes. The war party sailed to Rivers Inlet and was becoming discouraged because they could not find the enemy. But on their way two forward scout canoes encountered a group of Heiltsuk (Bella Bella, another Northwest Coast tribal group) who told them that the Bella Coola had barricaded their houses. The Mamalelekala canoes had been behind the others and when they arrived one of the Mamalelekala men killed the steersman of the Bella Bella canoes. The Kwakiutl then attacked and killed all the Heiltsuk. The Bella Bella men had been chiefs and hamatsas, and they had their ceremonial red cedar bark and hamatsa whistles with them. It was from this encounter (murder) that the Kwakiutl acquired what became the most important of the winter ceremonial dance societies —the hamatsa society—which we describe later. The Kwakiutl canoes returned home, satisfied that they had accomplished a great deed.

The village at Gilford was abandoned for many years after the raid. Some of the surviving Koeksotenok moved to Kingcome with the Tsawatenok. Most survivors moved to Village Island with the Mamalelekala because a large number of Koeksotenok had already been living at Village before the raid and the marriage ties between the two tribes were strong.

Beyond defensive maneuvers and ceremonial functions, tribes had only minimal corporate reality. They were, however, bonded together by a common mythological tale of origin. The Koeksotenok, for example, shared the following tale of origin:

The first Koeksotenok man came from a cedar tree. His name was *Hawilqwolas* "one who comes from the cedar." He changed his name later to *Tsɛeiqami* (Tseikami), "Supreme" or "Head-Winter-Dancer."

Q'aniqilaq[u] "Transformer" arrived at Islet Point by canoe where Tseikami was residing. Tseikami's son, *Tisamgit*, invited Transformer for food. Transformer was going to roast his salmon, and saw that Tseikami's children were roasting the same kind of salmon, Sisiutl [double headed sea serpent]. He was amazed that they could catch and eat the drippings of the Sisiutl without harm.

Transformer put Tseikami through many trials. He put a rock around Tseikami's neck and attempted to drown him. Tseikami went under and Transformer started to walk away, satisfied that Tseikami was dead. He reached a certain distance, and heard singing behind him. When he turned around he was amazed to see that Tseikami was alive and singing. Later Transformer put Tseikami in the fire and when there was nothing but ashes remaining he departed, satisfied that Tseikami was dead. He reached the same distance as before and again heard singing. When he turned around he saw Tseikami was alive and singing. Transformer changed Tseikami into a Saw-bill duck, but the latter was able to turn back into human form. After many such trials Tseikami and Transformer became friends as equals because Transformer could not vanquish Tseikami.

After his trials with Transformer, Tseikami returned to Viner Sound with his daughters. Qolus "Thunderbird" was up on the mountain and, looking down, saw Tseikami's fair daughters. He liked their looks and descended from the mountain. After making his face human by removing the Thunderbird headpiece, he sang a song before Tseikami. He asked and received permission to marry one of Tseikami's daughters. Qolus removed his Thunderbird cloak and commanded it back to the mountain. He then became fully human. It is from the union of Thunderbird and one of Tseikami's daughters that the Koeksotenok descended.

The Kwakiutl recognized one social unit larger than the tribe—the confederacy. This was nothing more than a cluster of loosely knit, informally related neighboring tribes who interacted among themselves more often than with other tribes. The Four Tribes of Gilford constituted such a confederacy; they came to Gilford during the winter, each living in a special residential area within the village, and they tended to potlatch and intermarry among themselves. Confederacies today, however, have little meaning beyond the fact that members of the Four Tribes still tend to intermarry among themselves.

Other significant changes have also occurred in Kwakiutl social organization. The rank-class system has broken down and numimas are no longer important to the Kwakiutl. Concomitantly, descent is no longer traced ambilaterally; the Kwakiutl have adopted the Canadian-American bilateral system where a child is equally affiliated with the kinsmen of both parents. This shift in the descent system is related to changes in their kinship system. As revealed in Table 4, for example, the Kwakiutl traditionally referred to their sisters and all female cross- and parallel-cousins by the same term, waqwa. They referred to their brothers and all male cross- and parellel-cousins by the term nimwiyut.[5] This form of nomenclature is known as Hawaiian cousin terminology. Today, for the most part only the older Kwakiutl know or care about the traditional kinship system. The terms currently used are a rough approximation of those used by Canadians and Americans. Now members of the village often label other people as a cousin or as a distant cousin without being able to trace precise kin linkages in such a way as to demonstrate the relationship. Anyone who is in approximately the same generation as oneself and who is thought to be related in some way is designated as a cousin; anyone at approximately the parent generation who is considered to be a kinsman is called an aunt or uncle.

Kwakiutl social organization has undergone other notable transformations as well. Traditionally, after marriage the bride and groom moved to the groom's father's community (patrilocal village residence), and indeed, they usually lived in the father's big-house (patrilocal household residence) as part of an extended family. Technically the bride and groom could move to the village of either set of parents (ambilocal village residence), or, for that matter, they could settle

---

[5] A cross-cousin is either mother's brother's child or father's sister's child; a parallel-cousin is either mother's sister's child or father's brother's child.

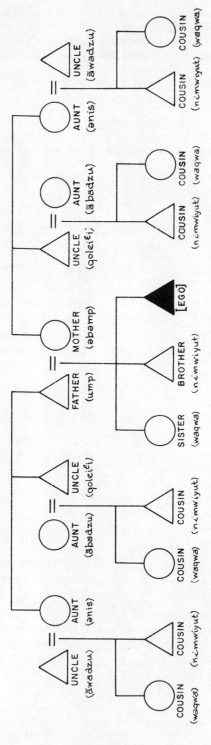

American-English and Kwakiutl Kinship Terminological Systems

in the groom's mother's village of birth. The decision was generally made on the basis of primary numima affiliation. That is, if a man had the right to claim a position in the numima of either his father or his mother, he and his bride typically moved to the community where he claimed the highest rank. If the bride outranked the groom, they could live with her parents; as the system worked, however, the Kwakiutl preferred to, and more often did live with the groom's parents. Today the Kwakiutl do not necessarily move to the village of either parent, and they prefer setting up their own independent household (neolocal village and household residence)—although in fact many of them do live with one or another set of parents for a least a brief time after marriage.

Even though the Kwakiutl had no obligatory marriage prescriptions, they tended to marry outside their own numima and often outside their own tribe in order to bring new and important names and privileges into one's own numima. Occasionally, however, a nobleman was encouraged to marry within his numima in order to perpetuate symbols of rank within his own line. He might, for example, marry his younger brother's daughter, or a half-brother could marry his half-sister if they had different mothers. Sexual relations between a man and his brother's wife were regarded as offensive, but through the custom of the levirate he could marry her if his brother died. It was considered bad form for the children of siblings (first cousins) to marry. Even today there is some feeling against this. Ernest Amber, for example, remarked to Roberta Drake, "Gee, I wish you weren't my first cousin. I could really go for you." Roberta was noticeably disturbed by the suggestion. Nevertheless, first cousin marriages do occur today.

The ideal marriage among the Kwakiutl was between a man and a woman of equal rank, especially if both were noblemen in the line of primogeniture in different numimas. Marriage among the nobility was arranged by the parents of a young couple; the boy and girl might never have seen each other before. Marriage arrangements were cloaked in the strictest secrecy—even excluding the young couple until the final details had been worked out—because rival families might try to break it up. Rivals could, for example, pay a young man to make love to the girl and persuade her not to marry her betrothed, or they could pay her to say that she had fallen in love with another man.

Boas (1966:53–55) summarizes the principal elements of traditional Kwakiutl marriage among the nobility.

Aside from this fiction [that a wife is obtained in war from a foreign tribe], marriage is conducted on the basis of the potlatch. Setting aside minor details, an agreement is first reached between the parents or, after their death, by those who assumed the parents' responsibility. The payment to be made to the girl's parents having been agreed upon, a binder is paid by the groom's representatives. When the number of blankets settled upon has been accumulated by loans from the groom's [numima], the bride price is delivered to the house of the bride's father. In addition to the stipulated price, blankets are paid to call the princess and to still others to "lift the princess from the floor of the house." Then the bride is handed over to her future husband's party and her father gives her husband blankets to represent her mat ($le'we^\epsilon$), food, and household goods, such as boxes, baskets, dishes, and spoons needed by the young couple. The value of these is often almost, if not quite, equal to the price paid. In some cases, the bride's father gives at the same time a copper (*sayabala*^{ε}*yo*), names and privileges to his son-in-law, but ordinarily this payment is deferred until a later time, generally after the birth of a child, when "the repayment of the marriage debt" takes place. This does not consist of blankets, but of "bad things, trifles," which include food, household goods of all kinds and particularly a copper, names and privileges which are handed over in the "privilege box." The value of the goods paid at this time is far in excess of what the bride's father has received. It is important to note that the only payment in the recognized standards of value is made by the groom. All the return payments are in objects.

The fiction that the marriage is one between two tribes or villages is maintained throughout. The groom's party is said to arrive by canoe, and when repaying the marriage debt, the father-in-law is supposed to arrive on a catamaran—two canoes tied together and covered with a platform of planks. The mast of the catamaran is the copper (*Lak·E*^{ε}*ye*) given to the son-in-law.

After the repayment of the marriage debt, the obligations of the contracting parties have been fulfilled, and the marriage is ended. If the young wife continues to stay with her husband, she stays "for nothing," which is not dignified. A new contract has to be made in the same way as the first one, but the payments are generally much less. The whole matter seems to be a little more of a formality, although proud and rich people may make the same extravagant payments as they did in the first marriage. In the records of marriages in which many children are born, there are no references to this attitude, although the principle of the end of the marriage after the repayment of the marriage debt is clearly in the minds of the Indians. The repayment of the marriage debt may be delayed for several years and the children born during this period receive names and privileges from their maternal grandfather. Undue delay of the repayment of the marriage debt is liable to cause trouble. When a certain man seemed to evade this duty, his son-in-law had an image representing his wife carved. At a feast to which he had invited the people, he put a stone around the neck of the image and sank it in the sea. Thus he blemished the rank of his father-in-law.

Often, after the annulment of a marriage through repayment of the marriage debt, the woman is married to another man. After four marriages, her high rank is established, and it seems to be assumed that after this she should stay with her last husband.

The advance in social rank arising from the potlatch features of the marriage often overshadows entirely the primary object of a marriage, namely, the establishment of a family. Instead of this, the transfer of names and privileges becomes the primary consideration, and fictitious marriages are performed, the sole object of which is the transfer of names, privileges and property previously described.

The marriage system described by Boas no longer exists in its traditional form. The last arranged marriage at Gilford was in the 1940s; no one in the village today between twenty-one and thirty-five had his marriage arranged but more than 60 percent of those who are thirty-six or older, excluding common-law alliances, did have. Several villagers in recent years have rebelled at the attempt of their parents to arrange their marriage. Benjamin Otter, for example, recounted his behavior in 1945 when he discovered that his father was trying to make such an arrangement with the family of a girl whom he did not know. Benny ran away from his home at Turnour and started working in a logging camp. His father attempted to stop him by pulling back on the stern rope of the gill-netter as Benny left the float. But when he saw that he could not do it, his father shouted to Benny, "Don't come back, you dog!" (Calling a man a dog in Kwakwala

A chief's daughter with her aba-
lone ear pendant and incised
silver bracelets—both symbols
of wealth (E. C. Curtis)

Chief holding speaker's staff and
ceremonial rattle (E. C. Curtis)

is one of the worst invectives in the language.) A few days later Benny's brother-
in-law, a chief from a neighboring tribe, came to the camp where Benny was
working and told him that he should go to Gilford on Saturday, but he would not
tell him why. Later that week Benny returned to Turnour Island to pick up some
things he had forgotten. He had another argument with his father and returned
to the camp. Again, Benny was told to go to Gilford. This time, on Friday, he
complied. That evening his father instructed him to have dinner with a certain
family, along with some other guests. Agnes Abel was cooking, but neither Agnes
nor Benny knew they were betrothed and were to be married the following day.
Only Benny's father, his mother having died at childbirth, and Agnes' parents
knew of the arrangements. That night Benny conceded to get married as his
father wished. But he did not discover that Agnes was to be his bride until the
following day.

Church weddings and civil ceremonies in the Indian Agent's office are
now the most popular form of marriage, although unformalized common-law
unions are also frequent. Even those people at Gilford whose marriages were
arranged and who went through the traditional Indian ceremonies—"Indian marriages," as some Kwakiutl call them—later had their union formalized by either
a church or Agency wedding. Benny and Agnes, for example, were later married
by the Agency Superintendent. The transition from Indian to White marriage
ceremonies was not abrupt. At first, of course, the Kwakiutl followed their own

customs. Later the Indian ceremony was followed by some form of White man's service. Now, however, the sequence is reversed. Indians are first legally married according to Canadian law and then they may have a potlatch.

A wedding took place at Kingcome during our year of fieldwork. The bride and groom were first married by an Anglican minister. Following this service the newlyweds, their families and guests went to the community hall for the wedding reception which was actually a modified potlatch. In order to facilitate the bookkeeping of the 200 visitors, Kingcome residents were directed to the right side of the hall, visitors to the left. The chief whose funeral service was described in Chapter 3 spoke in Kwakwala giving the history and rank of both the bride's and the groom's family. As part of the marriage debt, the groom's father gave a wallet of money to the bride's father which was to be distributed at another potlatch the following day. Following this, the chief spoke at length, giving marital advice to both the bride and groom. Then another ranking kinsman of the groom spoke about the history of both families. He too gave advice to the newlyweds and thanked the guests for coming. Few people appeared to listen to these speeches; children ran around and adults talked among themselves.

Several Tsawatenok danced in button blankets while the speakers beat rhythm on the floor with lengths of wood. Following this a Tsawatenok woman gave advice to the bride and groom. Immediately afterward a small group of people began assembling gifts to be distributed among the guests, and shortly thereafter food was prepared. Thirty cakes were lined side-by-side on a table along with a one-hundred-pound wedding fruitcake. The newlyweds sat quietly behind the table with some friends and relatives. One of the officials passed out paper cups for drinks and others distributed sandwiches. Kinsmen of the newlyweds reportedly bought 100 loaves of bread to make the three or more sandwiches each person received. Three or more apples and oranges were passed around next to each person. By the end of the evening Jeffrey Hardy had a pasteboard box full of cake, sandwiches, apples and oranges. Most guests, however, put their food in the paper bags that were circulated for this purpose.

After the food had been distributed several women passed out crocheted doilies made by the bride's family. All women present received waterproof nylon scarves. Immediately following the distribution of gifts the first speaker—the ranking Tsawatenok chief—spoke about the exchange of a copper between the two families. By 10:15 P.M. guests began to leave and an Indian dance band was set up. Children were taken home and the adults danced and celebrated until 3:00 A.M.

The following afternoon the potlatch was continued by another family as a part of the commemorative ceremony for someone who had died. Villagers, especially women, danced in their button blankets to the rhythm provided by four men sitting at the far end of the building behind a four-foot plank. The ranking chief in yesterday's ceremony gave a brief oration in potlatch-Kwakwala and then, on two separate occasions, relatives of the deceased distributed towels and pillow cases to the approximately one hundred fifty assembled people. Later the same chief called the names of men to receive money in rank order according to their potlatch position, and he publicly announced the amount each was to receive from the wallet in yesterday's wedding ceremony. The wallet contained approximately $350. Representatives of the Mamalelekala received first; Gilford received second and the Nimkish of Alert Bay received third. Some of the men were given $10, and at least one was given $20. Others were given $2 in addition to, in some cases, a handmade quilt. After the money had been distributed the chief of the Village Island Band gave a lengthy speech thanking the host and acclaiming his background and generosity.

Contemporary spouse choices tend to come from within the village at Gilford (village endogamy), and also from within the Band, but numima and tribal affiliation of one's spouse is now essentially irrelevant to mate selection. As we observed earlier, however, most spouses are still drawn from among the Four Tribes, reflecting the continued close contact among, especially, the Tsawatenok, Koeksotenok and Hahuamis. Two wives at Gilford came from Bands other than those represented by the Four Tribes. Consequently they have no preestablished social or kinship ties within the village, and as a result, they tend to be peripheral to the major social relations there. Alien people intermittently express a desire to leave the village, and shortly after our period of research, both of these wives and their families moved away.

The Potlatch

In Chapter 2 we described the potlatch as a public display and distribution of property in the context of one individual or group claiming certain hereditary rights or privileges vis-à-vis another group. While this statement suggests the general nature of the potlatch, the actual mechanics of the potlatch are more complicated than that description intimates. Potlatches may be described from an alternative point of view as a congregation of people who are invited to publicly witness and later validate a host's claims to or transmission of hereditary privileges, and to receive in return, each according to his rank, differential amounts of wealth.

Potlatches were given at critical life events: birth, adoption, puberty, marriage, death. They were given as penalties for "breaches of ceremonial taboo such as laughing, stumbling or coughing at winter dances" (Barnett 1968:36). Face-saving potlatches were closely related to penalty potlatches. They were, in Barnett's (1968:36) words, "prompted by some accident or misfortune to one's self or a member of the family. The capsizing of a canoe, a bodily injury and the birth of a deformed child" were all appropriate occasions for a face-saving potlatch. A third category of potlatch was the competitive, rivalry or vengeance potlach. These were extravagant, ostentatious contests with property, each claimant trying to give away or destroy more property than his rival and thus establishing his right to a contested privilege or position.

An essential feature of all types of potlatches was its public nature. The host, with the support of his family, numima or tribe, invited other families, numimas or tribes to act as formal witnesses to his claims.[6] The potlatcher traced

---

[6] Usually a family invited a family; a numima invited a numima, or a tribe invited a tribe. The host group did not receive gifts at a potlatch.

his line of descent and his right to the claim. No name, dance, song or other privilege could be used without having it publicly acknowledged and legitimated by the attendants of a potlatch. Since only people of substantial wealth could afford to potlatch lavishly or often, rank and wealth were but counterparts of each other—one implied the other. Under no circumstances did a host invite his guests as witnesses to an announcement or a claim without feasting them or distributing some form of property. In general the more grandiose the display of wealth, the higher was the prestige of the donor. Boas (1966:51), in fact, took the position that the principal motivation of Kwakiutl behavior was the desire to acquire prestige and respect. From the guests' point of view, a potlatch was a festive occasion, a time for entertainment and feasting.

As we observed above, potlatch guests received different amounts of property according to their rank. The same serial ordering held true at feasts where guests were called to be seated at special places of honor. Drucker and Heizer (1967:45–46) describe what they call the invariable distribution-sequence at potlatches.

Gifts were given first to the chiefs of the highest ranked guest tribe, beginning with the first chief of the highest ranked numima of that tribe, then proceeding in order with the other chiefs of his numima. The second chief in rank of this tribe, that is, the first chief of the second ranking numima, was the next to receive his gift, and his numima brother chiefs were given gifts in sequence, before beginning with the third ranking chief and his numima, and so on through all the numima of the tribe. Then the highest ranking chief of the second tribe in precedence was given his gift (following the lowest ranked position in the first tribe), and the same order was followed, numima by numima, before beginning with the third tribe.[7]

Drucker and Heizer (1967:46–47) continue to describe quite a different principle of ordering at feasts.

In a seal feast given to the Kwagyuł confederacy, for example, the first chief of the kwagyuł (gwetᵉla) was served a seal breast. Then the first chief of the kwᵉxa, the second tribe in rank, was served a seal breast, and a like portion was served to the first chief in rank of the walas kwagyuł. (The extinct q'omkutis were supposed to have preceded the walas kwagyuł.) Next, the second ranking chief of each tribe, in the same tribal sequence, was served a seal flipper, the third ranking chiefs, likewise in sequence, were each served a similar portion, followed by the fourth chiefs in rank. The remainder of the seals were distributed generally to the lower ranking chiefs. If the main dish of the feast consisted of some .other food, the chiefs were called forth to be seated at the named decorated feast dishes in the same sequential order. If the guests were of a single tribe, as, for example, the nimqic or the mamalele-qala, the first chiefs of the numima were served in order, then the second chiefs, following the numima sequence, and so on. The same sequence was followed on certain other occasions, such as that of speech-making at the sale of a copper. Logically this feast sequence seems to conform better [to] the Southern Kwakiutl concept of relative rank in the expanded guest group than does the potlatch gift order.

---

[7] Not all Northwest Coast scholars agree with their description of serial giving at potlatches. Some would argue that gift giving conforms more with Drucker and Heizer's description of the ordering principle at feasts given in the following paragraph.

As suggested in the preceding passage, guests not only received in rank order, but there were marked inequalities in what they received. High ranking chiefs received more valuable property at a potlatch than lesser ranking men, thus providing each participant with a comparative standard against which he could measure himself vis-à-vis other recipients. The value and quantity of gifts distributed at a potlatch reflected not on the guests but on the donor. It reflected his wealth, rank, generosity, and the esteem in which he held himself. It also reflected, over time, the power and prestige that he would be able to maintain over other high status men. In addition, each man tried to return as much or, preferably, more than he received on a prior occasion.

Potlatch materials included a wide range of goods, including Hudson's Bay blankets, money, canoes, coppers, flour, kettles, dishes, sewing machines, tables and, in former times, slaves. A ranking Nimkish chief gave an extravagant potlatch at Village Island in 1921. The following excerpt tabulates the range and quantity of goods that were distributed.

> The second day a *xwe'xwe* dance with shells was given to me by the chief of Cape Mudge. I gave him a gas boat and $50 cash. Altogether that was worth $500. I paid him back double. He also gave some names. The same day I gave Hudson's Bay blankets. I started giving out the property. First the canoes. Two pool tables were given to two chiefs. It hurt them. They said it was the same as breaking a copper. The pool tables were worth $350 apiece. Then bracelets, gas lights, violins, guitars were given to the more important people. Then 24 canoes, some of them big ones, and four gas boats.
>
> I gave a whole pile to my own people. Return for favours. Dresses to the women, bracelets and shawls. Sweaters and shirts to the young people. To all those who had helped. Boats brought the stuff over from Alert Bay to Village Island by night. (This was to evade the Agent [because potlatching was illegal at the time].) This included 300 oak trunks, the pool tables and the sewing machines.
>
> Then I gave button blankets, shawls and common blankets. There were 400 of the real old Hudson's Bay blankets. I gave these away with the *xwe'xwe* dances. I also gave lots of small change with the Hudson's Bay blankets. I threw it away for the kids to get. There were also basins, maybe a thousand of them, glasses, washtubs, teapots and cups given to the women in the order of their positions.
>
> The third day I don't remember what happened.
>
> The fourth day I gave furniture: boxes, trunks, sewing machines, gramophones, bedsteads and bureaus.
>
> The fifth day I gave away cash.
>
> The sixth day I gave away about 1000 sacks of flour worth $3 a sack. I also gave sugar.
>
> Everyone admits that was the biggest yet. I am proud to say our people (Nimpkish) are ahead, although we are the third [in the Kwakiutl rank structure], *Kwag·uł*, *Mamalelqala*, *Nəmgəs* [Nimkish]. So I am a big man in those days. Nothing now. In the old days this was my weapon and I could call down anyone. All the chiefs say now in a gathering, "You cannot expect that we can ever get up to you. You are a great mountain." (Codere 1961:470–71)

Coppers were among the most prominent and important of treasure items at traditional potlatches, especially in the transfer of privileges at the time of marriage. Coppers are large pieces of beaten sheet copper cut into the form of a shield with a T-shaped ridge running down the middle of the bottom half.

They were painted with black lead, and a design was incised through the paint. Coppers were associated with wealth and have been loosely compared with thousand dollar bills in Canadian-American currency. Each copper had a name, and its potlatch history determined its value. For one copper which was named, "All other coppers are ashamed to look at it" 7500 blankets were paid. Another copper called, "Making the house empty of wealth" was worth 5000 blankets; and, "Steel-head salmon, i.e., it glides out of one's hand like a salmon" was purchased for 6000 blankets. Each copper was valued at the cost required to buy it, and it increased in worth at each transaction.

Potlatches were associated with every important change in social status— birth, marriage, death, among others—and they were the medium through which one's status could be changed. The acquisition of a new name in a potlatch, for example, signalled a change in status. Newborn infants were given a name, often the name of the place where they were born. A naming ceremony for low ranking people was modest, but it was often of substantial magnitude for ranking members of the tribe. The infant was given a second name at ten months. According to Barnett (1968:28), in recent times kerchiefs were distributed to men and children who witnessed this bestowal. The child received a "young man's name" a short time after his ten-month name. Only young men received the kerchiefs this time. When he was about sixteen or seventeen the youth received still another name in a "paint-giving-away name" ceremony. Only unmarried men participated and each received a shirt. Finally, blankets were distributed when the young man

Chief holding copper, "takes every-thing out of the house." The copper was valued at five thousand blankets (E. C. Curtis)

assumed adult status. Only men who themselves had gone through the ceremony and assumed a "spread-out name" could participate. It was at this point that a man began to acquire important potlatch names and privileges from his father.

We have already noted that death inaugurated an important series of potlatches. These occurred not just at the time of death, but could be given intermittently over several years in commemoration of the deceased. Such a potlatch was given at Turnour Island in March of our year in the area. Approximately 400 people from Gilford, New Van, Village and Alert Bay congregated at Turnour to attend the potlatch given by Brian Seaweed of Turnour Island and William King of Alert Bay. Brian gave the ceremony for his mother who died a year earlier; William gave his part because his son and daughter-in-law had come back together again. Kingcome villagers were not invited to this potlatch because William intended to go there and continue the potlatch later.

Fifty people from Gilford arrived shortly before noon, in time for dinner. The meal was served in a recently built, modern styled community hall. It consisted of beef stew, bread, butter, coffee and tea. After dinner the tables were folded up against the wall to make room for the performances which began at 3:10 P.M. when Gilbert Johnny of Fort Rupert took the speaker's staff. All the speeches that day were made in formal or potlatch Kwakwala. Gilbert thanked the people for coming and he told why the potlatch was being given. Chief Cesaer Walas of Turnour introduced the next event: men singing and drumming, and women wearing button blankets in mourning for the deceased. After a brief delay four songs were played, one with the women dancing.

Someone gave Brian Seaweed a small copper "to wipe away the tears." Brian received the copper and "mourned." A chief from Fort Rupert took the copper from Brian and gave a speech. The copper was then passed to a woman who spoke and handed it to Chief Walas. Brian's sons appeared from behind the screen at the far end of the building and stood by Cesaer while the latter spoke. After his talk Cesaer disappeared behind the screen. A man from Blunden Harbor spoke about the history of the copper which had once belonged to Brian's great-grandfather. The story associated with the copper dealt with its being used for bathing people and curing their injuries. While the man from Blunden talked, another man brought out a covered box which was also to help remove sorrow. The box was ceremoniously taken away by one of the Seaweeds: he approached the box, reached out his hands to receive it and then withdrew them. He turned in a circle a couple of times and then repeated his reaching gesture. This sequence was repeated three times before he took the box, walked around the false fire in the middle of the room and exited through a door.

Chief Walas spoke again with the speaker's staff in his hand. He said the old ways such as songs, dances and potlatches must continue. "We must hang on to the old ways."

Brian Seaweed and Cesaer Walas went on stage where Cesaer applied eagle down to the heads of the nine men on the stage behind the long "drum" and the one bass drummer. Cesaer passed out red bands to be worn on the heads of all special men at that end of the hall, including a White couple from Seattle who are professionally interested in Kwakiutl dances and who had been especially invited to perform at the potlatch. Brian gave head bands to selected individuals sitting on the main floor. Then Brian, one of his sons, Cesaer and two other men danced. They passed completely through the hall, out the door by the wood stove and shortly reappeared without Brian's son. The drums on stage beat time to their dance.

At 4:30 P.M. sandwiches and coffee were passed out to everyone present and the potlatch was adjourned until 6:00 P.M. The first performance after supper was the Raven dance. Brian's son came around the fire in hamatsa dress which consisted of red cedar bark rings crossing his shoulders and a red head band around his forehead. Cesaer spoke briefly. Since this was only a practice session for the main events of the evening, the audience had dwindled to about twenty-five.

The potlatch reconvened at 7:00 P.M. with nearly 200 people in the hall. Holding the speaker's staff, Chief Walas in hamatsa attire spoke behind a microphone which had just been set up. The chiefs of the attending tribes beat the rhythm. Cesaer called out names, and Brian distributed money to the chiefs on the platform. The White man also received money as a special guest and performer. About ten minutes later Brian distributed packages of Players cigarettes to the same people to whom he had given money. Whistles were blown off in a distance, and by 7:20 all the seats were taken; children were sitting on the floor. There was a continual undertone of conversation throughout the rest of the evening.

At 7:30 a hamatsa initiate danced around the fire and then exited. A man from Kingcome emerged wearing a button blanket. He danced with Brian and others. Several women in the audience stood beside their seats swaying their bodies to the rhythm. The Raven appeared next, danced briefly and a second Raven appeared. They danced, one at each side of the fire. In certain poses (for example,

An episode in the Turnour Island potlatch

A village man dancing in his thunder-bird mask (Courtesy of National Defense, Canada)

when kneeling) one called to the other and the second answered, both vocally and with a clapping of the beak of the mask. Each Raven had a second person watching and following him around the hall. The dance itself involved a continuous fast rhythm and a constant change of head and body movement. Their feet followed the rhythm but their hands and head did not perform the same

Hamatsa (Cannibal dancers) inside the big-house at Gilford (Courtesy of National Defense, Canada)

movements. The hamatsa initiate reappeared and was immediately taken away by two men. Brian Seaweed began shaking his rattle and a hamatsa whistle sounded in the back room. Brian sang his own accompaniment. Then various people gave speeches and some women danced.

After a pause the Mountain Goat Hunter dance was performed. The Mountain Goat Hunter is supposed to capture the goat with a snare. He went off stage, returned and exited again. Cesaer Walas spoke and then Jeffrey Hardy from Gilford danced his hamatsa dance. His dance roused everyone in the room off their seats and as Jeffrey exited everyone shouted "whooo." The audience is asked to rise and be seated twice during his dance. Gilbert Johnny spoke. A man and a nine-year-old boy danced a hamatsa dance followed by the entrance of a Raven. The nine-year-old boy and the two men reappeared; the boy followed one of the men around the room, danced and copied his movements.

There was a brief intermission while apples were passed to the audience. The drums began again and six children ranging in age from two to six came out, some wearing button blankets, some wearing towels as blankets and some in plain clothes. A group of women in button blankets appeared, exited and reappeared. A man stood and mimicked the women, causing a great deal of laughter. An old man was called from the audience. He asked the audience for a knife. One person said he had one, but the old man ignored it and danced to me, speaking in Kwakwala and gesticulating toward me. I did not know how to respond because I did not know what he wanted. The crowd roared with laughter and after a few moments he went away. I asked my neighbor what it was that the old man wanted. He explained that the man had wanted a knife to cut the women open in order to see what was inside of them.

Cesaer explained in Kwakwala that the next dance was to be performed by the White couple who had been especially invited to dance the hamatsa. He then broke into English for the first time in the evening and said that "for you people who speak English the next dance is a surprise." After the couple danced there was a general round of applause for their performance.

After a pause the Ermine dance followed; Cesaer spoke again; then the Ermine mask reappeared, this time on a woman. At 9:30 Brian appeared wearing the same Ermine cape and mask and danced. Cesaer Walas took the cape and mask from Brian and performed. A man appeared in a blanket and performed a parody of the Ermine dancers. This finished Turnour Island's part of the potlatch.

Fort Rupert dancers performed next. There were many repetitions of the same dance—especially the hamatsa—by the same and different people. The men on the platform continued singing and beating rhythm. There were three hundred people in the hall. Those in the back of the room milled around restlessly and the crowd began to disperse. The children became very restless, wrestling among themselves, throwing things and making noise. At 10:20 P.M. three women did the Moon dance, two in masks and one without. Finally at 10:55 P.M. Cesaer Walas said that the midnight snack would be served. Mugs were distributed to the men, cups and saucers to the women and glasses to the children. Sandwiches, deviled ham on commercial white bread, were passed around. Sheet cake was passed out twice, cupcakes once and coffee twice. Cesaer announced that the cups, mugs and glasses were to be kept as part of the potlatch. Sixty gallons of oulachon grease were arranged on the floor for distribution. Each gallon jug of grease was valued at $5.00. Pieces of fabric, hand towels, dish towels, crochet doilies and anti-macassars, "shiny paper" pillows, commercial pillows, several stacks of dishes, plastic pails and dishpans were also distributed. A Sisiutl (the fabled double-headed sea serpent) with a raven carving was given to one of the men in the rhythm section on the platform. Apples were distributed among the children. Most gifts were distributed to women. Evelyn and I received a glass fruit bowl, a frosted white cereal bowl, two crochet doilies, fresh fruit, a mug, and cup and saucer. The grease was given to special male guests. Money was given only to men. I received $1.00; many men received anywhere from $1.00 to $7.00.

According to later reports Brian Seaweed gave $400 away in cash plus an unknown quantity of goods. William King gave away $300 and continued the potlatch at Kingcome with another $100. It was also reported that someone from Fort Rupert distributed $400 in cash and about $300 in goods.

Traditionally, all ceremonial occasions were marked by exacting standards of etiquette and proper behavior. Impropriety, whether accidental or intentional, required an immediate response. Such breaches of correct behavior as a mistake in ceremonial procedure, public quarreling or an accident witnessed by others, brought on a sense of shame and indignity. Payment was not always lavish but, as the Kwakiutl say, the offender must "cover (or wipe off) the shame" and re-establish his self esteem. Very often blankets were torn into strips and each witness was given a piece.

The Kwakiutl responded in a comparable way to insults. Occasionally pot-latchers deliberately insulted a guest by calling his name out of order, by spilling oulachon oil on him at a feast, by throwing him his gift or by presenting him with an inappropriate portion of food. The offended guest retaliated immediately. He distributed property or very frequently he destroyed it as· he made a negative reference to the potlatcher. Violence, however, is reported to have sometimes erupted. On some occasions the offending host chose not to recognize the face-saving efforts of his guest. This often precipitated a rivalry potlatch between the two men. Usually, however, mistakes were unintentional. Even though the Kwakiutl relied heavily on "potlatch secretaries"—men who knew the correct rank placement of each participant and who maintained a record of the property distribution—errors were made. A host or his speaker would unintentionally call out of order the name of a guest, or misseat a guest or serve him incorrectly. If the host did not catch his error right away, the offended guest restored his own pride by giving the host a reprimand gift. The host was embarrassed by his carelessness and made a restitution in double the amount of the reprimand gift.

Rivalries developed when two men competed for the same name, song or other privilege. Each contestant tried to demonstrate his right to the claim by reciting his closer genealogical connection with it and, of fundamental importance, by outdoing his rival in the amount of property that he could distribute. When one of the competitors reached the point where he had no more property to give away he had to admit defeat. It is in the context of rivalry potlatches where the Kwakiutl reached their greatest destruction of wealth. One competitor would "break" his copper, that is cut off a piece, thereby destroying its value, and give the piece to his rival. The rival then had to bring out a copper of at least equal value and break it, perhaps giving both pieces back to his opponent. The greatest merit came to the man who threw his whole copper into the sea, "drowning it." Such ostentatious destruction of property showed a man's utter contempt for property—the implication being that the small amount he destroyed was of little concern to him. Canoes, house planks, blankets and, at one time, slaves could be destroyed. On other occasions oulachon oil could be poured onto the fire until the flames scorched the roof planks and the clothing of the rival who was forced to sit impassively or admit that his competitor had wealth enough to make him uncomfortable.

The witnesses to these dramas acted as the judges. Ultimately it was they who decided who the victor was. One man of high power and prestige could sway public opinion by recognizing the claim of one contestant over the other at a subsequent potlatch. Indeed this fact points out one of the basic principles of Kwakiutl potlatching: a successful potlatch in itself could not legitimize a man's claim. Rather, it was the behavior of other hosts who recognized his claim at later potlatches that validated his claim. The individual who demonstrated the strongest hereditary right to the claim, however, was usually the winner of the contest.

Drucker and Heizer (1967:104–106) give an excellent illustration of competition between two ranking Kwakiutl.

> Ed's [Whonnuck] mother's father . . . was the direct descendant of the original Kwagyul eagle, since one of his forebears was the man responsible for the shooting of the kwexa [eagle] speaker in the kotink$^{\underline{w}}$ episode.[8] Ed's grandfather had only one heir, the daughter (Ed's mother); and according to the informant Whonnuck, his grandfather made it understood in his later years that he intended that she should inherit his eagle name and place, although he did not formally present her as his heir in a potlatch. He gave various names and other privileges to Ed's father in repaying the bride price, including some of the ceremonial privileges from his Awikeno grandmother, but the eagle place he did not transfer. When he died his daughter gave a mortuary potlatch at which she announced that she was the heir of her father's eagle place and took the name of doqwa'is. For a time she was not active in the place. Her intent was to give a major potlatch to place her son (the informant) in it.
>
> Her father had a kinsman among his paternal relatives who was a "younger brother," who through other relationships had inherited a minor or low ranking place, although still reckoned as a chief's place, in the tribal potlatch order. This individual was actually the closest surviving male relative of the deceased eagle doqwa'is. He therefore gave a potlatch to the kwagyuł, the kw$^\varepsilon$xa, the nimqic, and the mamaleleqala in which he announced that he and only he was the proper heir to the late doqwa'is, his "elder brother." Henceforth, he said, he would respond when the honorific name "doqwa'is" was called in the potlatches to the chiefs of the kwagyuł tribes and would gratefully accept the gifts given to him in his proper position as second in rank of the Kwagyuł eagles.

---

[8] Traditionally the Kwakiutl recognized one rank higher than a chief. Men occupying this position were known as Eagles, and they had the privilege of receiving before chiefs at potlatches. It was for this Eagle position that Ed Whonnuck's mother and his grandfather's "younger brother" were competing.

Now this was a rivalry potlatch, in the sense that the giver was announcing a claim to rights that he knew perfectly well were contentious. In realistic terms, the "uncle's" legal rights were weakened somewhat at Kwakiutl law because he was not a real "younger brother" of the dead eagle but only a terminological one. Thus his rights as an heir were inferior to those of a direct descendant. His hole card was the generally recognized fact that, as Mr. Nowell put it, "the chiefs did not like to have women [take important roles] in the potlatch." He had given various potlatches in his lower ranking place, demonstrating his solvency and his knowledge of the duties of a chief. He therefore hoped the chiefs would decide the matter in his favor.

Ed's mother, however, had been well indoctrinated in the customs of the potlatch. She in turn gave a potlatch to the several tribes, repeating the assertions of her rights. She demonstrated her knowledge of the traditions by recounting them in detail. Then she ordered one of her father's expensive coppers to be brought out. She paid an important chief of the kwᵉxa to bend the copper over just above the "T" and paid other prominent chiefs to mark cuts symbolically with chisels, without actually cutting pieces from the copper. Then she ordered one of her kinsmen to tow it to the sea behind a canoe and to cut it adrift in deep water and let it sink. "This is my gift to you, O chief," she said to her rival.

The "uncle" immediately sent for a very valuable copper that he possessed. When his kinsmen brought it from his house, he had the copper cut into pieces in the traditional way, giving fragments to the guest chiefs, except for the "T" or crosspiece, which he nominally presented to his "niece" in unflattering terms, and then went down to the beach to hurl the object into the sea.

Technically the uncle at this stage was ahead on points, so to speak, for the copper he had broken was more valuable than that sunk in the sea by doqwa'is. But then something else happened. "We had a lot of good friends," Mr. Whonnuck said. "Dan Cranmer's people, Charley Nowell's [elder] brother, and a lot of other important chiefs all said they would give my grandfather's real daughter all their coppers and all their blankets, until she made her "uncle" go broke. Her nimkish uncle [mother's brother] sent for a very valuable copper he had, saying that he would give it to her if she needed it.

"These things among the Indians," Mr. Whonnuck went on, "are just like White people in politics. It is just like a [White] politician running for election—he has to have a lot of friends so he can get a lot of votes."

While Whonnuck's appraisal may be a bit *simpliste* as far as modern Canadian politics goes, we still like it because it casts light on a crucial point in the resolution of conflicting claims. The announced intent of several important and wealthy chiefs to back Ed's mother resolved the case in her favor. Their avowed reason for supporting the woman was one based on the prior right of a direct descendant over a remote kinsman, even though the former was a female. The informant's statement makes the real reason clear: his mother played a better game of politics. The so-called uncle was beaten at that point; he could not possibly hope to muster enough wealth to compete with the combined resources of the several chiefs, so he simply dropped out of the picture as far as the eagle place was concerned.

Winter Ceremonials

Summertime among the Kwakiutl was the Bakoos season, the nonceremonial, profane, or secular part of the year.[9] This period usually lasted from March to November when individual families and numimas were at their summer

---

[9] The orthography of Kwakiutl terms in this section follows, for the most part, that of Hawthorn (1967).

fishing stations or in some other way occupied with economic pursuits. The Tsetseka or ceremonial, supernatural season extended from November to March. The Kwakiutl returned to their winter villages then, and members of the secret ceremonial societies devoted themselves exclusively to the winter dances, feasts, potlatches and other ceremonial activities. No work was done that was not necessary for survival itself or for the ceremonials. The transition from the Bakoos to the Tsetseka season was marked by a four-day interval of festivities during which time the deaths of those who had passed away since the last ceremonial season were commemorated.

The entire social organization of the Kwakiutl changed during the sacred season. New ceremonial names were used and new songs were sung; the use of Bakoos names was forbidden, and serious penalties were imposed on those who neglected or forgot this prohibition. Tsetseka was the season when supernatural spirits came to initiate the young into different grades of dance societies. The whole social system was altered to conform to the individual's relationship with the spirits. Drucker (1955:163) describes the winter dances as "cycles of dramas revolving around a single theme: the protagonist's encounter with a spirit who kidnaps him, bestows supernatural powers upon him, then returns him to his village, repeating the experience of the ancestor from whom the performer inherited the right to the performance." And according to Boas (1897:431), the object of the winter ceremonial was to "bring back the youth who is supposed to stay with the supernatural being who is the protector of his society, and then, when he has returned in a state of ecstacy, to exorcise the spirit which possesses him and to restore him from his holy madness."

The right to membership in the prestige graded dance societies—the totality of which comprise the winter ceremonial—was inherited in the same way as other rights and privileges, that is, through one's parents or as part of a dowry from one's father-in-law at marriage. As we described with the Bella Coola raid, the right to membership could also be acquired by killing a man in another tribe who possessed it. The prerogative of claiming a particular place in one of the dance societies was as personal and individualistic as a potlatch name. Dance society membership corresponded closely with the composition of the nobility, but even a nobleman had to assume his right to a position by going through formal initiation. Commoners were excluded from important participation in the ceremonials because they could not be initiated into any of the dance societies. They were, in effect, an impressionable audience to the ritual and theatrics of the initiated.

During the Tsetseka season, the tribe was bisected into two groups, the initiated and the uninitiated. The initiated, in turn, were divided into two societies, the Seals and the Sparrows. Sparrows, who were the managers of the ceremonial, provided comic relief by mocking and teasing the Seals who were under the influence of the spirits. Women could not officiate in the Sparrow society even if they were in the line of primogeniture (Boas 1966:179).

Members of the winter ceremonial dance societies were rank ordered. The Seal society maintained the highest position. They were seated in the place of honor at the rear of the big-house. Among them, the highest ranking hamatsa claimed the ranking seat in the middle rear of the big-house. Other members of the Seal society such as the Bear dancers, sat on either side of him. The Nutlamatl (Fool dancers and messengers of the hamatsa) sat at the far end of the Seal society; the Killer Whale and Rock Cod societies, the singers, sat in front of the Seal society. In addition the song leader, drummer, and herald, among other hereditary personnel, each had his seating place. Each society followed its own format and ritual, but all of them used certain ceremonial symbols such as red cedar bark head bands and neck rings, eagle down on their heads to symbolize peace, and red or black facial paint.

Kwakiutl dance societies comprised four major groups, the most complex and important of which was the hamatsa society. As described by Hawthorn (1967:46),

[Hamatsa were] under the supernatural inspiration of Bakbakwalanooksiwae, a powerful man-eating spirit, represented in the dance by the cannibal dancer or Hamatsa in human form. The second group was under the inspiration of Winalagilis, the war spirit initiator. The third group, the Atlakim dance series, could be used either for the Klasila [the four-day period preceding the Tsetseka season] or for Tsetseka display by changing the symbolic decorations. The fourth group was made up of the Dluwalakha dancers (meaning "Once more from Heaven")—those who had been given supernatural treasures or dloogwi, which were passed on to the novice, but who were not, as a group, involved in the convincing and terrifying displays of supernatural seizure.

According to Hawthorn (1967:39), the whole winter ceremonial was in a sense staged as a dramatic theatrical production. The intention of the initiates was to convince the uninitiated that the spirits and supernatural really were present within the village. Hawthorn (1967:39–42) continues with an excellent synopsis of the winter dances:

The house itself was a stage, with seating arranged so that the wall next to the curtain was shielded, and the dancers could come and go unseen. The central fireplace was the focus of attention. Dancing took place around the fireplace—the dancers moved four times around, counterclockwise, pivoting at the front and the back of the house, then disappeared. The performers entered suddenly through the front door, while others left unnoticed.

Illusion was managed in many ways. "Prop" men hidden above the beams of the house manipulated the strings that helped the dancers to control their magic tricks. Supernatural birds or other creatures, announced by thunderous noise on the roof, flew down through the air, appeared to pick up a person, and then flew up again. Underground passages increased the repertoire of magical tricks; such illusion gave credence to the presence of spirits. Curtis noted that some people even stayed home in the deserted village during the summer berrying and fishing times in order to prepare the tunnels under the floor of the Ghost Dancers' House.

Staging was always deliberate. Even the apparently spontaneous destructive frenzy of the Hamatsa was subject to planning (Curtis 1915:179): "He advances on lines which have been secretly marked out on the floor, and those who have been previously warned by the initiator that hamatsa will bite them sit where these lines touch the edge of the open space, so that hamatsa can easily reach them."

During the winter dance season the whole village, not only within the houses but also outside, become the scene of the pageant. A novice was sought after and

"Wild man of the woods" emerging from the forest (E. C. Curtis)

captured on the edge of the woods. Another novice—balanced on boards over a low-slung canoe—arrived apparently dancing on the water. The use of illusion was an important element: one novice was seen arriving by canoe with his sponsor when there was a sudden accident, the canoe overturned, and the novice was drowned. He was later revived and danced amid general rejoicing. Actually the drowning figure was a cedar carving which was weighted down and sunk. In another example of illusion the Hamatsa novice, fleeing to the woods, apparently disappeared in mid-

Ceremonial dancers in mythological bird masks (E. C. Curtis)

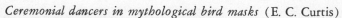

flight. The Hamatsas, wearing red cedar bark head and neck rings, went into the woods to capture the novice. On the way they were handed hemlock boughs, which they donned. They advanced toward the Hamatsa novice, who, in order to mystify the village spectators, quickly substituted red cedar bark ornaments for his green hemlock rings. When the crowd opened, he had apparently disappeared, quickly to reappear at a considerable distance in the person of a second substitute dressed exactly like him. This one was then surrounded and "lost" in the same manner (Curtis 1915:174).

In one part of the drama, the Hamatsa novice rushed out from the house with everyone else in pursuit. The Killer Whales, who had been teasing him, ran to take refuge in the water, where they were cornered by the novice. He was afraid to go into salt water, and they were afraid to come close to him for fear of being bitten. Several novices of the sea-creature spirits appeared for initiation at the edge of the ocean as though they had just come up from its depths.

Terror, drama, and comedy were balanced to produce good theater:

During the feast the grizzly bear may become aroused, growl and roar, and try to get out of the room.

The people scramble back to their seats along the walls, while attendants rush over to restrain the beast. After a terrific struggle, despite their efforts, a board will be torn loose, and they will all be sent sprawling, but instead of a grizzly bear the figure of a decrepit old man will totter forth (Drucker 1940:207).

Some dancers acted as buffoons and created a disturbance. Some were clumsy; some were mimics who staggered around imitating the actions of others:

While the real dancers are making their secret preparations behind the screen, the jesters amuse the audience. They dodge behind the screen, parody the coming performance. Or one may accuse the other of lying, then peek behind the screen and come out to report "the real truth" to a convulsed audience (Olson 1940:A:5, 175)."

Meticulous attention to the details of theatrical illusion and dramatic impact characterized the productions of the ceremonies.

Within the large plank house, the central fire cast lights and shadows. At the far end opposite the entrance door was a theatrical curtain made of wooden planks or muslin with the crest of the initiating spirit of the dancing house painted on. Behind the curtain, awaiting their cues, were the dancers in costumes. At one side was a small hidden cubicle to which the novice retreated. There were several such small rooms for the various dancers.

The dancing house in which the Tokwit dancers were going to perform was vacated and carefully guarded several days before the initiation. Underground passageways were dug, down which the dancer could disappear. A system of kelp speaking tubes was installed. Elaborate gear was brought to the house, such as false-bottomed chests in which the dancer would be concealed while apparently being consumed by fire.

Every opportunity to create drama was exploited. Here is an example cited by Drucker in a description of a Dluwalakha dance (1940:207):

"*The novice . . . flies away for four days, descends again, is caught and dances four nights like the rest. On the fourth night, the master of ceremonies . . . is bade to call the dancer's spirit down from the sky. He stands under the smoke hole, shouting his request that the "honored one from heaven" descend to show himself to the people. He tries very hard. Suddenly there is a tremendous thud on the roof, a blare of spirit horns, and a commotion at the door. The master of ceremonies sends the attendants to see if the spirit he has been calling has arrived. They report that there is something strange and terrifying without. They assemble at the door, holding their blankets out to form a screen, then back in. All at once they break away, revealing the spirit—a naked dancer, painted black, wearing a hominoid mask. The spirit dances, enters the cubicle, and is sent away when the novice is purified.*"

During the dances various tricks were employed to create convincing illusions. An apparent beheading used portrait carvings and bladders filled with seal blood. The fire thrower handled burning embers in leather gloves with wooden palms skillfully put on by his attendants. He walked on the fire over wooden boulders wearing protective footgear. The Tokwit dancer climbed into a wooden box, was consumed by fire, and in due course was reconstituted.

Curtis (1915:212–13) described two other examples of illusion, summarized as follows:

"*Kinkalatlala walks about the house, making her cries. A noise is heard, and a wooden kingfisher appears. The bird descends to the dancer and follows him, darts at him and spears him with its long beak. It then flies up to the roof. The dancer has strings which raise and lower the bird, and there is a man above on the roof who also controls the strings.*

"*The female Mitla spirit produces salmonberries out of season. Four masked female attendants dance around her. Salmonberry shoots are let down from the roof. The berries are pebbles covered with resin gum dyed with iron oxide. The people eat them and pretend to fall dead, but are then revived.*"

A simple device was the use of the dancer's blanket to aid in concealment. A gesture of a blanket-covered arm would make a screen behind which one mask could be changed for another, or a whistle held under the blanket could be blown secretly.

These dramatic winter ceremonials are no longer produced, but the Kwakiutl still sing the same songs and perform the same types of dances, wearing finely carved, painted masks, button blankets and red cedar bark neck and head rings. The performances, however, are not embedded in the ritual context of a rank stratified system where only certain people have the exclusive right to use particular names, sing specific songs, perform certain dances. The dances today are severely abbreviated versions of what they once were; dramas that originally took an hour or more to complete are now typically performed in a matter of minutes. The use of tricks and illusions, and almost all theatrical props such as false bottom chests, kelp speaking tubes and underground passages have disappeared. Currently anyone who has the skill and knowledge can perform any dance. In addition, the Indians execute their dramas in novel contexts. That is, dancing is still an important component of potlatches (and here people who have the legitimate prerogative to claim specific dances tend to perform them), but the Indians are also beginning to popularize their art during, for example, the summer tourist season in Alert Bay and when a dignitary such as the Lieutenant Governor of British Columbia visits the villages.

Many Kwakiutl are developing a renewed interest in their traditional art forms and other indigenous customs such as carving, painting, dancing and perhaps noncompetitive potlatching. Some of this revitalization is due to the enthusiastic response of White consumers. Different aspects of traditional Kwakiutl culture are well enough preserved so that they may be revived and maintained, but with reformulated meaning. The Kwakiutl are unlikely to reproduce their former heritage, but essential elements from the past along with syncretisms from the present may be perpetuated in the future as a distinctively *Kwakiutl* life style.

References and
Recommended Readings

*BARNETT, HOMER G., 1968, *The nature and function of the potlatch*. Eugene: Department of Anthropology, University of Oregon.

BOAS, FRANZ, 1897, The social organization and secret societies of the Kwakiutl Indians. *Report of the U.S. National Museum for 1895*, Washington.

*————, 1966, *Kwakiutl ethnography*. Chicago: University of Chicago Press. Helen Codere, (ed.).

*CODERE, HELEN, 1950, Fighting with property. *American Ethnological Society*, Monograph No. 18.

*————, 1961, Kwakiutl. In E. H. Spicer (ed.), *Perspectives in American Indian culture change*. Chicago: University of Chicago Press.

*CURTIS, EDWARD S., 1915, The Kwakiutl. *The North American Indian*, Vol. 10, Norwood, Conn.

DRUCKER, PHILIP, 1940, Kwakiutl dancing societies. *Anthropological Records*, Vol. II, pp. 201–230, Berkeley: University of California Press.

————, 1955, *Indians of the Northwest Coast*. New York: The Natural History Press.

*————, 1965, *Cultures of the North Pacific Coast*. San Francisco: Chandler Publishing Company.

*DRUCKER, PHILIP, AND ROBERT F. HEIZER, 1967, *To make my name good: a reexamination of the Southern Kwakiutl potlatch*. Berkeley: University of California Press.

*HAWTHORN, AUDREY, 1967, *Art of the Kwakiutl Indians and other Northwest Coast tribes*. Seattle: University of Washington Press.

*McFEAT, TOM, 1966, *Indians of the North Pacific Coast*. Toronto: McClelland and Steward Ltd.

OLSON, RONALD L., 1940, The social organization of the Haisla. *Anthropological Records*, Vol. II, pp. 169–200. Berkeley: University of California Press.

*ROHNER, RONALD P., 1967, *The people of Gilford: a contemporary Kwakiutl village*. *Bulletin 225*, Ottawa: National Museum of Canada.

*SPRADLEY, JAMES P. (ed.), 1969, *Guests never leave hungry: the autobiography of James Sewid, a Kwakiutl Indian*. New Haven, Conn.: Yale University Press.

*WOLCOTT, HARRY F., 1967, *A Kwakiutl village and school*. New York: Holt, Rinehart and Winston, Inc.

---

* The starred items in the bibliography are particularly recommended.